GIDEON CALDER

HOW INEQUALITY RUNS IN FAMILIES

Unfair advantage and the limits of
social mobility

SHORTS INSIGHTS

First published in Great Britain in 2016 by

Policy Press
University of Bristol
1-9 Old Park Hill
Bristol
BS2 8BB
UK
+44 (0)117 954 5940
pp-info@bristol.ac.uk
www.policypress.co.uk

North America office:
Policy Press
c/o The University of Chicago Press
1427 East 60th Street
Chicago, IL 60637, USA
t: +1 773 702 7700
f: +1 773 702 9756
sales@press.uchicago.edu
www.press.uchicago.edu

© Policy Press 2016

British Library Cataloguing in Publication Data
A catalogue record for this book is available from the British Library.

Library of Congress Cataloging-in-Publication Data
A catalog record for this book has been requested.

ISBN 978-1-4473-3153-7 (paperback)
ISBN 978-1-4473-3155-1 (ePub)
ISBN 978-1-4473-3156-8 (Mobi)
ISBN 978-1-4473-3154-4 (epdf)

Cover design by Policy Press
Front cover: image kindly supplied by Alamy
Printed and bound in Great Britain by CMP, Poole
Policy Press uses environmentally responsible print partners

To Kristian and Megan, with love and thanks

Contents

List of figures

List of tables

Preface

Each December since 2013, the UK's Social Mobility Commission[1] has published a State of the Nation Report. Each time, the headlines have been gloomy. Family background remains a highly reliable predictor of how we do in life, where we end up, and how long we live. The 2015 report reaffirmed that there is a wider gulf between the life chances of rich and poor than in any other nation belonging to the Organisation for Economic Co-operation and Development. Britain has the closest link between parents' earnings and those of their children among major industrialised countries. And 'those who rise to the top in Britain today look remarkably similar to those who rose to the top half a century ago' (Social Mobility and Child Poverty Commission, 2015b). We are a brand leader, a global exemplar of social immobility. And everyone seems to find this scandalous. Stories of an uneven playing field and a divided country, still starkly fissured along class lines, have a mysterious unifying power. For politicians of almost all persuasions, and for newspapers across the spectrum from *The Guardian* to the *Daily Mail*, this is an outrage. A tragedy. A blight. A waste of talent, a cooking of the books, a rigging of the game in favour of the already privileged. It is not OK not to be affronted by it. Yet social immobility persists, or worsens. The apple still falls close to the tree. Inequality, it seems, runs in families.

This book has two main aims. One is to explore that relationship between social immobility and the family, in both factual and ethical terms. Because family circumstances wield such an influence on how our lives go, they are deeply implicated in the transmission of unequal life prospects down through the generations. And yet most of us think that family life is – usually, in most respects – a valuable thing, and perhaps uniquely so. So there seems to be a tension between the urge to promote more equal life chances, and on the other hand the motivation to respect and protect the rights of parents and children to benefit from family relationships.

The book's other, slower-burning aim is to argue that social mobility is not all it's cracked up to be. In 2010, Gordon Brown, then UK prime minister, wrote that 'social mobility is not an alternative to social justice – it *is* modern social justice' (Brown, 2010 – emphasis added). The whole gist of this book is pitted precisely against this equation. If social *immobility* (or as I'll usually be calling it, 'class fate') is a problem, social *mobility* is not the answer to it. Instead, the priority should lie in reducing inequality itself. And indeed, reducing inequality between families is also the best way to tame the ethical tension between family life and equality of life chances. If inequality runs in families, it's not just families themselves that are pushing this along. The wider shape of those inequalities is just as crucial a factor. Much of the shoving power in the transmission of inequality through the generations lies in the nature and scale of the gaps between those with more and those with less.

Here, cosy harmony ends. If it seems everyone thinks that social immobility is bad, there's little consensus that reducing the gap between rich and poor is the best way to address the problems it poses. Perhaps the most important job of this book is to show that if we don't like the ways in which inequality runs in families, we need to think about how far families should be allowed to serve as vehicles for unfair privilege – and also, about how much of a gap we are prepared to allow between those on different rungs of the social ladder.

Gideon Calder
June 2016

Note

[1] As it was renamed in 2016; formerly, it was the Social Mobility and Child Poverty Commission.

Acknowledgements

Among many other debts I am grateful to my colleagues at the Centre for Social Policy at the University of South Wales (where I worked while writing this book), at the journal *Ethics and Social Welfare*, in the South Wales Equality Group and on the Newport Fairness Commission – and to Victoria Pittman, Ruth Harrison and the editorial team at Policy Press for their efficiency and friendly prods. I'd like to thank Arabella Calder and Jenni Calder, who read parts of the manuscript in draft. I owe a great deal to the students – from first-year undergraduates to PhD researchers – with whom I've grappled with the kinds of question that emerge here. And to Jurgen De Wispelaere, Anca Gheaus and Steve Smith, for all the insights and critique and helpful steers bobbing up in the everyday flow of working on recent projects together. Kristian and Megan Calder got me thinking about all this, and it's a joy (though tiny, next to that which they bring) to dedicate this book to them. Regrettably, any mistakes in it are my own, and – let's be honest – not really attributable to any of these people.

Parts of Chapters Two and Four are adapted from my article 'Family autonomy and class fate', *Symposion: Theoretical and Applied Inquiries in Philosophy and Social Sciences* 3(2): 131-49. I am grateful for permission from the editors to use that material here. I am grateful too to Miles Corak for permission to reproduce Figure 3.1, originally in Corak (2013) and to the Sutton Trust for permission to use Table 3.1, which is based on work originally published in Machin et al (2005).

ONE

Introduction

In 2014, the Social Mobility and Child Poverty Commission published a research report on how children from disadvantaged backgrounds fare in the education system, compared to their privileged peers. It includes various graphs and charts depicting the relation between socio-economic status and the likelihood of, for example, achieving the expected level at each stage of the journey through school, and getting into an elite university. One, when I read it, stood out:

Figure 1.1: School performance and class background

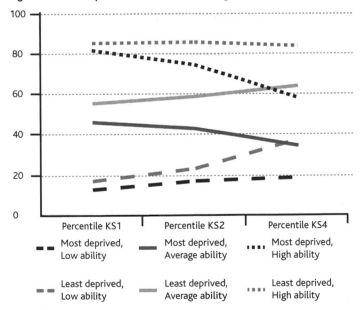

Source: Adapted from Crawford, Macmillan and Vignoles (2014, p 9)

Its story is shocking. This is not because it necessarily comes as a surprise. We may roughly know this picture already. It shows a world we grow used to inhabiting, without knowing the numbers. The shock here lies in the sheer starkness of those lines, and the steady directions they take. If this book were a film, and this diagram were its trailer, two things this graph tells us would boom out in the voiceover. First: kids born rich and poor start out more or less equally 'smart'. (Or more specifically, the high-attaining poor kids are achieving roughly on a par with the high-attaining rich kids at the age of five. Pre-school achievement is evenly distributed across class divisions.) Second: between the ages of 5 and 16, the rich kids pull substantially ahead. By 16 the lowest-attaining rich kids have overtaken the poor kids initially categorised as having 'average ability'. And across the same timespan, the average ability rich kids overtake the highest-attaining poor kids. At the age of sixteen, these gaps are still expanding. These are state school children: the picture does not include those in fee-paying education. Here, now, in the United Kingdom, how well kids do at school is strongly linked to how well-off they are. It's the same in all other developed countries too. But it's especially true in the UK – a country in which officially, of course, every child matters, and where a commitment to equality of opportunity is, ostensibly at least, part of the non-negotiable fabric of the kind of society we like to see ourselves as being. To say this picture reflects in any simple way what the children concerned *deserve* seems a basic kind of error. Children can hardly be said to have earned their different fates. They are visited upon them, via what has come to be known as *intergenerational inequality*: the handing down and maintenance of social advantage and disadvantage. Thus that diagram conveys a very basic, very drastic kind of unfairness.

This book is about different versions of this unfairness: the shapes they take, and the reasons why they are unfair. It's about the relationship between the family, social mobility, and the very idea of equal life chances. And it's about how we need to think about equality, in order to take steps to improve that relationship. This is a complex, shifting package. For it's not just in educational achievement that this unfairness bites. It applies to work: the jobs we do, the fulfilment and status it affords. It applies to health: how much of it we have through life, and how long we live. It applies to housing: where we live, the type of home we live in and on what terms, whether we inherit property, and our chances of getting on the 'housing ladder'. Where we sit in each of these respects reflects the playing-out of tangled dynamics between the family and social mobility. So those dynamics are a matter of pressing concern.

They are also, as a matter for public debate, a sensitive, treacherous place to go. There are plenty of reasons for this. Three, perhaps, stand out. All reflect a kind of 'common sense' – in the particular way that Stuart Hall and Alan O'Shea use that term: 'popular, easily-available knowledge … customary beliefs, wise sayings, popular nostrums and prejudices' (Hall and O'Shea, 2015, pp 52-3). Viewed this way, common sense is the background of 'everyday thinking' we rely on when we say 'of course!'.

'Of course we do'

First, the family is – of course – politically hard to touch. We can hardly move for references to 'hard-working families', and for the connection of family ties and the domestic sphere to what is primary, secure and enduring in a world of flux. The 'wish to pass something on to your children is the most basic, human and natural instinct there is,' said UK Prime Minister David Cameron in 2015, pledging to 'take the family home out of inheritance tax' (Cameron, 2015). Thus a policy explicitly favouring homeowners is justified on the basis of a universal 'family instinct', intended to be classless in its resonance. No claim is made that family matters more to the posh than the poor, or vice versa. The 'naturalness' of the family coming first is presented as a kind of social unifier – even, as here, in the service of a policy which will shore up differences in privilege. It's *the* family' that matters, not this or that family, in these or those circumstances. Individual families are invoked as exemplars of this wider social institution. They are, this suggests, equal stakeholders in it.

Second, the value of social mobility is – of course – taken as a given. A slippery concept in some ways, it is worth defining twice over. In the pioneering 1953 work *Social mobility in Britain*, David Glass defines it simply as 'the extent of movement in social status or social position by individuals of diverse social origins' (Glass, 1953, p 5). In a recent study conducted for the Department for Business, Innovation and Skills, we find it defined like this: 'the ability of individuals from disadvantaged backgrounds to move up in the world' (Crawford et al, 2011, p 6). It has come to function as a constant motif, a common denominator in discourses from both political right and left. Less charged or contentious than 'equality', it has become, in its more abstract way, as unlikely as the family (or indeed, apple pie) to be panned as an idea.

Third, though the idea that every child matters equally, or deserves an equally 'fair go' in life, is genuinely held by most of us, most of us behave in ways that seem to undermine it. For example, in many of the most routine decisions that parents make, and the most everyday aspects of their relationships with their kids, those who look after kids make a mess of that notion that kids might have an equal start – and often, quite deliberately subvert it. This point might seem less emblematic of 'common sense'. But what's 'common sense' about it is not the experience of the gap between a genuine belief in equality of life chances and the things we actually do, but the sense that – of course – we're entitled to do those things.

More than that, we may see it as our *job*, as parents, as family members, as relatives, to prioritise our own, to boost their social mobility or (if they have started out privileged) to preserve their place on the ladder, to do all we can to maximise their chances of flourishing in life, to bequeath to them as much as we can. This is where our three items of 'common sense' coincide. In fact, there has been a kind of inflation here, in terms of expectations of what 'good' parents should be doing for their kids – of what is 'only natural'. Using economic language here is quite the point. As Megan Erickson puts it, 'The nurturing and raising of children, once seen as deserving of fierce protection from market forces, has now become intertwined with economic pressures: It is never too early to start equipping a child with the skills and personality traits that will ensure productivity and success in the global economy' (Erickson, 2015, pp 7–8). It's a responsibility, a pressure, that falls first and mainly to families themselves.

Hence, the meeting-up of our three common-sense values: 'family', 'social mobility' and 'equal life chances'. If it's 'only natural' to do whatever we can for our kids, it's going to be tricky at best for political discourse about social priorities to infringe on what families do to advantage their kids over others. But those same overlaps make for tensions. Promoting social mobility – this thing that conventional wisdom has down as *obviously* right, making people's backgrounds matter less in terms of predicting where they end up on the 'social ladder' – seems *by definition* to mean stopping parents advantaging their kids, or at least, putting pretty tight reins on it. And allowing parents to push their kids up the ladder seems to facilitate a process by which some families come to have, and to matter, more than others. It undoes the 'classlessness' of the appeal to family values, or the value of the family as institution. It allows for some families to profit at others' expense.

So these three items of common sense seem clearly out of joint. Something has to give. If it's really true that we want social mobility, it seems, its price must be an unsanctifying of the family, or a limiting of parents' entitlement to 'do the best for their kids'. This is not necessarily to reject conventional wisdom, or to be sniffy about it. Each of these items of belief has something in it. But the tensions between them invite us to get them in some kind of balance, or at least to allow them to cohabit a little more easily. If each is to be part of the furniture of a coherent account of social justice, we need to figure out whether, and how, they can be set in some kind of easier relation.

Outline of the book

Chapter Two takes a look at how the family fits into theories of social justice – or often, how it doesn't. Considering its emblematic status as a social institution, the family features less in political philosophy than we might expect it to. Instead, a cluster of questions around marriage, gender, privacy, care, the status of children, and the domestic sphere in general, have tended to be grappled with in critiques of the mainstream texts. But many of those critiques have now themselves become mainstream. Belatedly, via feminist theory, a mushrooming literature on the ethics of care, and the work of political theorists seeking to 'factor the family back in', we have built up a nuanced picture of how we might consider – for example – the entitlements of parents, and the limits of what they may do to influence or privilege the children they look after. There are difficult balances here. Family relationships offer, potentially at least, uniquely valuable things. They also carry unique kinds of threat, in the potential for abuse and manipulation. And they also, as we have already glimpsed, threaten to disrupt the realisation of a fairer society. They do this most when we most protect what gets called 'family autonomy': the right of families to make decisions on their own terms, and to forge their own priorities. The job of Chapter Two is to survey this terrain, and to see where that leaves us.

Chapter Three, 'Social mobility and class fate', looks more closely at the nature of inter-generational inequality. How reliably are social advantage and disadvantage transmitted from one generation of a family to the next? Just how fateful is 'class fate' – the predictability of where you end up in life, according to the social position of your parent or parents? And how does class fate actually happen? How much of it is cultural, and how much economic? Is it down to individual choices made by parents and their kids? Wider structural factors? Attitudes? Material constraints? Parenting styles? Behaviours and orientations picked up at school, or elsewhere outside the home? Or does it mostly come down just to money? To think this through, we need partly to think about what constitutes disadvantage and advantage in the first place – what it is to be better or worse off – and how inequalities in these respects relate to the playing-out (or not) of social mobility. In doing so, we find that things done under the auspices of family autonomy are indeed heavily involved with the transmission and cementing of class fate. But we also find a great deal of evidence that levels of material inequality are very strongly, sometimes *more* strongly, implicated.

In Chapter Four, our focus is mostly conceptual. Attention turns to equality of opportunity – one of the few principles we're all supposed to favour. I look at the usage of this term in political rhetoric, and then compare this with recent theoretical discussions of its nature and scope. By this stage, because of what has gone before, we are in a position to draw conclusions about the relationship between the three items of common sense picked out above. For some – including many in front-line politics – equality of opportunity is entirely distinct from equality of outcome, or (as I shall also be calling it) equality of condition. I dispute that view. Instead, I argue, genuine equality of opportunity is incompatible with persistent significant material inequality. As we see in tight focus when we look at the notion of 'meritocracy' and its shortcomings, equality of opportunity and equality of condition are best seen as interlinked, rather than as opposites. If this is right, a point emerging in Chapter Three is reinforced in a different way. Social mobility is nothing like sufficient, as a vehicle for social justice. Indeed, promoting it too much, or by itself, might pose clear impediments. This is a well-established view on the left, of far older vintage than the current tendency to think that social mobility is the answer to all our social justice problems. My aim is to make a case for retrieving it.

Chapter Five, 'Towards real equality of life chances?', warms to this theme. Equality of life chances is beginning to sound like a rather empty term, too often used quite cheaply. I consider one reason why this might be the case: that in fact, there is a strong tension between that value and others that liberal egalitarian theories of justice will endorse. This does not show that equal life chances are a false value, or not worth pursuing – but just that in doing so, we may need to compromise on others. Family autonomy is right in the frame here. We need to think about just how much leverage parents should be allowed to advantage their own children over others. We need to be explicit, in ways politicians would never be comfortable in voicing, about the ethical limits of family privilege. I make some modest suggestions as to how the levers of public and social policy might be used to achieve a fairer distribution of life chances.

In the closing chapter, I restate the overall case made in the book, in the form of seven brief summative conclusions.

In a time of unprecedented global challenges, questions about what we owe our descendants might come to greatest prominence when we think of climate change, or international security, or the scale of future population growth. I want to try to show that these questions matter just as much close to home, and in the most mundane aspects of our everyday building, nurturing and sustaining of relationships. It matters that we get the chance to do that everyday stuff. It also matters that this happens in ways which do not directly shrink the scope for others to flourish too. And it matters that future generations do not inherit the still-drastic class inequalities to which, at this stage of the 21st century, we're still very much in hock.

TWO

The family and social justice

[T]he family, while neglected, is *assumed* by theorists of justice.
(Okin, 1989, p 9, emphasis in original)

So wrote Susan Moller Okin in a widely influential critique of mainstream academic theorising of the fair society. Those debates were famously reframed and re-ignited with the publication of John Rawls's *A theory of justice* in 1971 (Rawls, 1999, revised edition). Rawls's framework for liberal egalitarianism became compulsory reading for anyone wanting to grapple with the deep questions of what social justice might look like. What kinds of rights should individuals have? What is the relationship between freedom and equality? Under what circumstances are we obliged to obey the law? What kinds of economic structure are compatible with social justice? What do citizens owe the state, and what does it owe them? Rawls's answers to these questions set a kind of unavoidable benchmark: an account of the 'basic structure' of a just society. It wasn't that you had to *agree* with his own, broadly social-democratic take on these issues, or his underpinning assumptions, or his method. It was just that you had to take his approach on board. From then on, few could get away for long, discussing theories of social justice, without sometime, somehow, invoking Rawls.

Yet Rawls's extended, rigorous account of the 'basic structure' says very little about the family. This seems anomalous. The basic structure refers to 'the way in which the major social institutions distribute fundamental rights and duties and determine the division of advantages from social cooperation'. These major institutions 'define men's [sic] rights and duties and influence their life prospects, what they can expect to be and how well they can hope to do' (Rawls, 1999, pp 6-7). Rawls gives as an example of a major social institution 'the monogamous family'. So the family is clearly, on his terms, something to which principles of justice should apply. This is a big point to make. By no means everyone with an axe to grind on questions of the family and social justice is happy with such talk. It's just that he doesn't, then, go on to tell us *how* justice applies to family relations, or what a socially just family might look like. '[G]iven that family institutions are just ...', he writes (Rawls, 1999, p 429), at the beginning of a discussion of the course of moral learning from childhood on. So he takes them as read. As Okin puts it, he works on the assumption of 'a family environment that is both loving and just' (Okin, 1989, p 108). He just doesn't tell us what this actually means, or what it is about a just society that ensures that this environment arises, or, as discussed further in Chapter Four, how the workings of the family as a vital sphere of human nurturance fit into the wider scheme of fair equality of opportunity. The family is just *there* in the structure of Rawls's just society, in its more-or-less modern western nuclear version, doing its work off-radar, sounding absolutely pivotal but at the same time deemed not to be in need of direct, sustained analysis.

So that's what it means to neglect and make assumptions about the family at the same time. It tends to prop up ideas about social justice without itself being interrogated. Rawls's case is not exceptional; his manoeuvring around the family has been fairly typical among political philosophers. But so what? What happens when we put the family back in to our understanding of social justice? What ripples does this cause, and what further questions does it raise?

In fact, it raises very many questions. Some are about rights, responsibilities and obligations: what may or must be done by or for other people *because* they are fellow family members. We'll return to these often as this book unfolds. But others concern the definition, or constitution of the family itself – and we do have to get straight on this to get started. What even counts as a family, and who should count as family members? Should our definition be relationship-based, so that the definition of a family depends on how we define kinship?

Or location-based, so that 'family' has to do with living together over an extended amount of time? Or should it be functional, so that 'family' is defined in terms of certain roles, or the social needs it fulfils, such as the upbringing of children? Or should we combine all three, so that a family 'unit' is constituted by a certain kind of cohabiting relationship, which carries out certain kinds of function? Either way, things quickly get complicated.

One basic reason for this is that family relationships come in so many different forms. The number of parents, the sex of those parents, the number of children, the biological relationship of those children to each other and to their parent(s) — all of these have enough routine variations to make it clangingly erroneous to presume as an archetype or default some kind of cartoon 1950s American model family with a picket fence. And if this was already so in America in the 1950s, it certainly is now, internationally. Imagine that family with a chisel-jawed dad and aproned mom, say in their mid-30s, standing outside their detached suburban home with two children, aged eight and five. Now think about what 'normal' has come to mean, and how we might need to edit that image, to make it more representative. For the first time on record, living with a parent has recently become the most common living arrangement among US adults aged 18-34 — overtaking living with a romantic partner (Fry, 2016). In the UK in 2015, 40% of young adults aged 15-34 were living with their parents (ONS, 2015). Cohabitation of kids and parents lasts ever longer. So depicting a typical domestic set-up, perhaps we should put some years on the people in our image. Let's make our cartoon parents 55, and the kids 27 and 24.

But should there be kids at all? The most common family type in the UK is a married or civil partner couple family without dependent children — there were 7.8 million of these, in 2015 (ONS, 2015). Are they families too? Of families with dependent children, 25% have lone parents (ONS, 2015). And all of these are rising too: the numbers of dependent children with same-sex parents; the number of children conceived via a sperm-donor; the number of children born via a surrogacy arrangement; the number of children living in reconstituted families (where one or both parents has children from a previous relationship). The point of all this is not to help refine our search for the ultimate, 'default', totally representative image of the family. It is to highlight that such an image cannot exist. Whatever defines the family, there is no single instance of it that is somehow authentic. There is a good deal more to say about the definition of 'family' than this, and about the very many ways, historically and now, in which families have been constituted. There is no simple definition of a family unit – in the dictionary, in law, or in policy – that captures all the senses in which we routinely think of family relations, whether nuclear or extended. Hoping for *any* kind of representative cartoon image may itself be a mistake.

Still, to use the term, we need to pin it down in the right kind of general way. The political philosopher David Archard offers this definition of the family:

> [A] multigenerational group, normally stably co-habiting, whose adults take primary custodial responsibility for the dependent children. (Archard, 2010, p 10)

This will do, for the purposes of discussing the issues that feature in this book. Importantly, the definition involves no need for a blood relationship: the children in question might be step-children, conceived by donated gametes, or adopted. Family-hood depends instead on a *custodial* relationship. And although our family has adults and children, there is no need for any particular number of either, or for the adults (if there is more than one parent) to be married. Of course, family relationships persist well after the kids have left home, and indeed formed new family units of their own. But our focus in this book is on the custodial relationship as Archard frames it. When we're saying here that theories of justice neglect the family, it is usually this relationship and its circumstances that we think are being neglected. When we're talking about the relationship between the family and life chances, it is this unit that we are referring to, not blood relations or an extended family network of cousins and great-uncles. Most of us are brought up in a multigenerational group of the sort described by the definition above. Our immediate question is: so what, in terms of social justice?

The next few sections highlight some of the ways in which questions of justice arise within families, and between families and other social factors and institutions.

Families and individual rights

A core element of theories of justice will be the nature and scope of individual rights. Rights are a kind of basic currency, particularly of liberal theories of justice. They denote our entitlements: what it is that individuals are entitled to, what others ought not prevent us from doing, and what we ought to be protected from. In light of this, a lack of focus on the family in theories of justice becomes especially striking. On the one hand, it will neglect a major sphere of human interaction, and the everyday social world – namely the domestic, or the sphere of 'normally stable cohabitation'. On the other hand, it will serve to obscure how it is that we become the individuals we end up being – just because families, for the majority who grow up in them, are typically so instrumental in that story. As Okin puts it, many theorists of justice 'take mature, independent, human beings as the subjects of their theories without any mention of how they got to be that way' (Okin, 1989, p 9). If we assume that the primary, most urgent questions of social justice are those that arise from relationships between adults, outside of familial contexts, this has ostensibly warping effects on our understanding both of the human condition, and of social life. The preamble to adulthood – the custodial backstory – is squeezed to the margin, if it is taken to matter at all.

This seems starkly awry, for various reasons. One is that maturing to adult individuality – 'getting to be that way' – is not automatic, or self-confirming. There are conditions of human development. Meeting them requires certain kinds of work to be done. On the face of it, this work seems as crucial as any going in society. As we will return to later in this chapter, it takes up a major chunk of a society's time and resources. To position that whole arena as somehow off-limits for the discourse of social justice seems arbitrary.

Another reason is that most of us think that if we are going to operate with a system of rights at all, at least some of these rights should apply to children as well as adults. Perhaps not in the same way, or for the same reasons. Perhaps there are some rights that apply only to adults, or others only to kids. But some of those rights for children will, specifically, impose constraints or obligations on parents. So the idea that in a lifespan spent only 'within' the typical period of family cohabitation – say, that of someone dying at 15 – no questions of rights might arise seems to miss the point. Some 'negative' rights, for example – rights that protect us from potentially harmful treatment by others (see Noggle, forthcoming) – seem to apply *especially* urgently to children, and sometimes more urgently the younger those children are.

A third reason is that so many of our encounters as individuals happen within a family context. Questions of justice are often taken as referring to the public sphere – the realm of strangers, with different, sometimes competing priorities, needs, values, abilities and so on. There is a tendency, as Nancy Fraser puts it, to 'depoliticize' the sphere of family interactions by consigning it to the sphere of the 'personal' or the 'domestic' (Fraser, 2013, p 62). But this move has been rendered untenable by consistent critique, often from second-wave feminists seeking to highlight iniquities and power imbalances in the division of domestic labour, but from a wide range of other directions too. We can no longer (if this were ever plausible) simply park the family in a private sphere, fully beyond the legitimate reach of legislation or public intervention. If there are indeed areas of family life where the state should not normally intrude, these need to be staked out and justified, rather than presumed (Archard, 2003, ch 3; Brighouse and Swift, 2014, ch 1).

Privacy and autonomy

So we need a conversation about what should be deemed a family's own business – which aspects of parent–child relationships should be regarded as beyond the proper reach of state action. In practice, although we find very different stances on these questions, they sit on the same continuum between extreme positions that virtually nobody occupies. It's hard to find anyone who will plausibly argue for total family privacy, such that the exertion of any kind of political authority at all would be an unwarranted intrusion into a family's own business. And we are equally unlikely to find anyone insisting on total state control of the domestic – and so a relinquishing of any form of parental authority at all. What we find instead are stances accommodating more or less intervention, or diverging over when intervention is justified. It's a matter of balance. There are periodic controversies about where to draw the line. Take Article 12 of the United Nations Declaration of Human Rights: 'No one shall be subjected to arbitrary interference with his privacy, family, home or correspondence' (United Nations, 1948). This is not a principle that attracts widespread scorn, or starts fistfights among theorists of social justice over whether it's worth supporting. But this is partly because of its openness to interpretation. Everything hangs on what counts as *arbitrary*.

And since parents are the ones most likely to be shaping family environments and steering the direction that families take, what we're talking about here is effectively the extent of the right of parents to make their own decisions about how to interact with and raise their children. So questions about the extent of a family's right to privacy are closely tied up with questions about what we might call family autonomy – or parental autonomy, if we're focusing on the rights of parents to be left alone to raise their families as they choose. And here, what counts as 'arbitrary' interference depends crucially on how we view the interests of children and parents, and the relative priority of each.

Take the following areas of decision making about children, where the decisions could rest either with parents or the state:

- ensuring that children have an adequately nutritious diet;
- ensuring that children are educated;
- the setting of an age of sexual consent;

- decisions about medical intervention, for example vaccination or organ transplant;
- the appropriateness of smacking or other types of corporal punishment;
- the adoption of a particular set of religious beliefs.

Running through a list like this makes clear the importance of drawing a line. It also highlights the drastic nature of any position seeking to draw that line in an absolute way, at either end of the continuum – so to recommend, for example, that the state withdraw from any role at all in family life. Taking that line would amount to a commitment either to a doctrine of extreme neutrality on what contributes to child welfare (so that the state must always sit on the fence rather than commend this or that mode of parenting practice); or a principle that the parent is always, by definition, right about what is in the child's best interests; or a principle that even if the parents sometimes get those judgements wrong, the state still has no right to intervene, regardless of how much harm it seems to be doing the child; or a principle that the interests of the child count for nothing against the interests of the parent to parent as they please. It would, in effect, mean that it would be solely down to the discretion of parents whether their children were fed or educated, when they first had sex and with whom, and whether they receive medical treatment. These seem, let's say, unlikely positions for anyone to take up. They would point to a kind of institutionalised indifference about how a society's children were getting on – not so much liberation from state meddling, as a recipe for neglect.

But as we get further down the list, we might find that the issues become more contentious, or that drawing a line becomes more difficult. While there is no buzzing parental lobby for the right not to educate one's children, there are plenty of people who think that recourse to smacking should be up to parents, rather than proscribed by law. And a proposal to deny parents the right to decide whether to steer their children into holding particular religious beliefs, or none, is difficult to envisage in an even moderately liberal society. What distinguishes these cases from each other? A key factor is the nature of the interests at stake. There is no coherent way to argue that it's in a child's interests not to be adequately fed or educated. Yet there are very plausible reasons to think that a child might have an interest in being invited to hold religious beliefs (though not to be indoctrinated into them). Those reasons are contestable, for sure. But whichever way you look at it, ending up a religious believer is not, in itself, a harm equivalent in scale to chronic malnutrition or missing out on education. Whether it is in itself a harm *at all* seems to depend on one's perspective.

For these reasons, there is a fair amount of bluster and hypocrisy in the language of those who making certain kinds of noises about family privacy, or think family autonomy is sacred. Any idea that there's something *inherently* wrong with meddling in a family's business, or that we should see the family as a cut-off and bounded safe haven in a world of threats and overweening do-goodery, is making two kinds of mistake. One we might call ontological – to do with the nature of the family itself, and its relation to the rest of the social world. No family is an island, somehow insulated from any interchange with wider social dynamics – economic circumstances, policies, dominant discourses, 'common sense', peer influences and general historical context. Talk of families as 'units' may risk reinforcing a false sense of atomisation. For reasons which, as we will see, matter greatly when it comes to social mobility, a family cannot, with the best will in the world, realistically steer its own pure course through the social landscape. Yes, families, and particularly parents, will wield considerable power over the way their story unfolds. But in light of all these other shaping factors, they are not sole authors. In a complex society, there is no such thing as an unhindered, or self-legislating, or unmonitored family.

The second mistake is normative. It concerns the *value* of being free. For to prioritise family privacy above all else, for example, would be to say that whatever goes on in the family realm – whether domestically, or out in the wider world – is acceptable as long as it is private. This would then include the private abuse of children by their parents or siblings, intimate partner violence, and indeed the manipulation or exploitation of elderly family members by their grown-up children.

This is not what defenders of the family as a private haven want to protect. Stepping down from that position means weighing up which intra-familial practices ought, and ought not to be, publicly regulated.

Everyone, wherever they stand on the continuum between privacy and public intervention, will find themselves tasked with that kind of appraisal. Often this seems to involve a deal of contortion. We pick and choose when we want to leave families be, in ways that leave fuzzy the ultimate status of family privacy and autonomy. Libertarians resentful of nannyish government regulation of school meals to ensure a more nutritious diet, or the imposition of rules denying parents the right to take their children on holiday in school term time, will not be averse to blaming a glut of antisocial behaviour on feckless parenting, and insisting that something be done. The press damned social workers for over-intervention in the Orkney 'child abuse' episode in the early 1990s just as readily as they damned them for under-intervention in the Baby P case in Haringey in 2007. And perhaps most glaringly, the strongest advocates of traditional (Judeo-Christian) family values – of, for example, an authoritative, patriarchal vehicle for the instilling of discipline and right thinking in children – will often, also, take the view that all of this is a means to the end of reinforcing social order and stability.

The following statement dates from 1985 – but it is retained, entirely intact, in the rhetoric of the contemporary 'Tea Party' right in the US, and its corollaries elsewhere:

> We should support the family as an institution. The family is a real alternative to the state, in fact a force for individual freedom and the first-line safety net for the welfare of the individual. It provides a bulwark against the encroachment of the state on the individual. Indeed, the quality of our citizenship is determined by the quality of our family life, and it is through the caring authority of parents that individuals learn to be independent. (Rogers and Clements, 1985, p 56)

And here is a passage from Brenda Almond's more recent case for 'the protection of the family as historically understood'. She argues that state help for vulnerable families has the effect of facilitating family break-up. Overly generous welfare provision makes accessible to everyone lifestyle options previously reserved for the rich. Factors such as:

> routine mandatory provision of independent accommodation and support for single parents ... have a tendency to nullify what might be called the 'market' aspect of setting up a family – the idea that, under free-market conditions, saving and sacrifice on the part of a couple is essential to provide, first of all, a roof and then reliable financial support throughout the process of child-bearing and child-raising. (Almond, 2006, p 195)

Do such points amount to a defence of family autonomy or not? On the one hand, the family is pitched as a realm and conduit of freedom. It should be *left to itself*. But on the other hand, this vision of its role is anything but neutral. It's not as if, for the fiercest defenders of 'family values', families are to be entrusted to do their business any old how, according to their own lights. Far from it. The family has pre-ordained jobs to do – to promote the welfare of the individual, to produce independent adults, to provide reliable financial support – and is valuable insofar as it completes them. In the picture we get from those most anxious to preserve the 'traditional' family, its freedom does not amount to the freedom not to improve the quality of our citizenship. Rather than being valuable in itself, family autonomy is exhorted as a means to that end. The most anxious advocates of 'family values' are hardly agnostic or *laissez-faire* when it comes to decisions made in the domestic sphere.

While there may often be a measure of hypocrisy in this apparent weaving and flip-flopping, simply pointing this out is too easy. These convolutions speak of conceptual hurdles which loom up regardless of the ideological direction from which one arrives at questions of family privacy and autonomy. In fact, nobody thinks that either is unconditionally valuable – immutably, or purely for their own sake, or regardless of circumstances or what families get up to. And if they are conditionally valuable – to be promoted in some senses or cases, but not in others – we can expect, as indeed we find, deep and complex disputes about where those lines are drawn.

Gender roles

Most work critiquing the neglect of the family in theories of social justice has come as part of wider treatments of gender – and *its* neglect in mainstream political theory up to the late 20th century. This neglect has various features. Prominent among them are these:

- *Talking as if people, or the people who matter, are men*: the assumption that the inhabitants of the political realm – the subjects of civic participation, decision making, transactions, deliberation – are men. Or if not men, then embodiments of stereotypically male characteristics, orientations and priorities. So theorists of the just society have either assumed than it's only male interests that are centrally at stake, or offered a kind of false neutrality, where they assume that male interests are somehow universal – that men 'stand for' humans in general.

- *A sectioning-off of the domestic or private sphere*: the assumption that questions of social justice concern the public realm – the realm of men and fathers – rather than also including relations within the family. So work that happens in the home, for example – housework, care work, the job of raising children, and other traditionally 'feminine' tasks – is regarded as somehow a given, or as naturally occurring, or as a customary default, rather than something to be recognised as part of the contestable subject-matter of justice for its economic value, political significance, or necessity to the architecture of civil society.

Combined, these features have meant that in the hands of political philosophers, discussions of social justice have tended (to echo Okin) both to neglect gender, and to assume it. They have neglected it by not addressing it directly, and by lack of attention to gender differences. And at the same time they have taken for granted the work that society has been most likely to associate with the feminine. The public realm is reflected here as shared in common – a space where citizens might meet on an equal footing, enfranchised to participate regardless of their individual circumstances. The domestic becomes affirmed as the sphere of particularity, difference, emotion: a protected space where the governing principles of the public do not, by definition, apply, and where we will expect people's experiences to be diverse, uneven, personalised, and very much their own business. And if this is a trait of theoretical discussions, this itself reflects stubborn real-world assumptions about how the family fits into the wider social landscape. To return to Fraser's term: this depoliticises the domestic. *Re*politicising it has, of course, been a priority in feminist critiques of political theory.

This itself has given rise to divergent lines of response, and sometimes deep disputes, among those seeking to get gender and the family installed at the heart of debates about social justice. Counteracting the first assumption, we find arguments both that universalised conceptions of citizenship are inherently flawed, precisely because they will never be gender-neutral (e.g. in Young, 2011), and that they might be redeemed by being made more genuinely inclusive (see, for example, Nussbaum, 2000, 2001). In response to the second assumption, some would seek to include domestic relations within the ambit of an expanded, more nuanced conception of justice (Okin, 1989). Others have identified a separate mode of discourse and practice associated with the category of our everyday, particular relations – not principles-based, as with justice, but care-based (on which, more shortly).

What's important for now is to establish that questions of gender are so tightly enmeshed with discussions of the family, relations within it, and its place in the wider social terrain that they infuse those discussions at every level – so much so, that it we might expect to find them kept in the foreground of a book like this. It may require some explaining, therefore, that this is not how things are going to go. When we move on, in the following chapters, to focus on social mobility and then on ideas of equality, we will not keep gender questions centre-stage.

When distinguishing between different social categories and groups, we will usually be working along the lines of class and income, rather than gender – or indeed ethnicity, or disability, or sexuality, or other factors that, if dwelt on, would illuminate critical dimensions of the architecture of social mobility. This is not, of course, to deny the value of that kind of illumination, or the sheer weight of those factors, either generally in terms of social justice, or specifically, in terms of how families work, and how the family links up with wider social issues. Rather, it is because of the way we're treating the family itself, in our working definition. Here, we're mainly interested chiefly in how families affect life chances, *regardless* of the genders (or ethnicity) of those involved.

That said, the prism of gender puts a spotlight on issues that are crucial to include, even in the briefest tour of the relationship between the family and social justice. Work done in the domestic sphere is an unavoidable example. As we've already seen, feminist lines of critique have been instrumental in highlighting how work done at home supports the rest of society while not being recognised – or paid. The division of domestic labour is still organised along traditional gender lines. There remains a stubborn, if now sometimes less overt, presumption that domestic labour will fall to women. So for example, in households with two different-sex parents where both work, daily housework remains far more likely to be done by women. So while the gender pay-gap is (slowly) closing, and more top-level jobs are occupied by women, the 'double burden', or what Arlie Hochschild called the 'second shift' remains typical (Hochschild, 2012). Thus women's growing importance in the paid workforce comes alongside an ongoing responsibility for housework and childcare. According to a recent study by the Institute for Public Policy Research (IPPR), '[t]he average time men spend on housework and particularly childcare has risen since the 1970s, but this has occurred mostly among men with higher levels of education. In recent years, moreover, the time women spend on childcare has also increased' (Lanning et al, 2013, p 4).

Against the wider backdrop of the family as a social justice issue, this matters in various ways. Some concern matters of *distribution*, and some of *recognition*. This helpful distinction arose out of theoretical debates in the 1980s and 1990s over how to understand injustice and disadvantage, and how best to compensate for these. The contrast was notably pinned down by Nancy Fraser (1997). Distributive elements of social justice are socioeconomic: those for which the chief focus is material resources, and the differences in opportunities and quality of life to which any distribution of income and wealth in society will give rise. Recognition-based elements of social justice are cultural: those for which the chief focus is identity and difference, and the ways in which perceptions of and discourses about these can reinforce patterns of social inclusion and exclusion. As Fraser puts it: 'The remedy for economic injustice is political-economic restructuring of some sort.... The remedy for cultural injustice, in contrast, is some sort of cultural or symbolic change' (Fraser, 1997, p 15).

Looking at the headline conclusions of that IPPR report, we can see how this distinction unpacks in the case of domestic work.

Despite some improvements in family policy in recent years, the combination of a relatively long period of maternity leave, meagre paternity leave, and a lack of affordable childcare for children under the age of three tacitly supports a male breadwinner model. The workplace reform agenda has sought to 'nudge' employers into better accommodating family responsibilities and as such has been predictably weak. The assumption that care is primarily the mother's responsibility is reflected in the assumption among some women that they should be 'grateful' if their partners are active parents. (Lanning et al, 2013, p 5)

There are clear questions of distribution here: parental leave and affordable childcare are resources distributable in different ways, more or less fairly. Childcare and housework done within families for those families are customarily unpaid. They are also a crucial element of any socioeconomic structure. Take them away, and that structure will buckle or collapse.

Childbearing, childrearing and housework are thus the prime examples of socially necessary labour that society prefers not to remunerate. This can be viewed as a form of exploitation, whereby society, particularly those not doing domestic work, directly profit from it being the responsibility of a particular section of society. In Annette Baier's words, 'the long unnoticed moral proletariat were the domestic workers, mostly female' (Baier, 1987, p 50). Children (we'll come back to this shortly) are a public good: all of society indirectly benefits from their existence, and from their growing up into adults. Children affect most of us directly, 'as parents, as grandparents, as practitioners and as tax payers' (Rutter and Stocker, 2014, p 1). But the costs of rearing them fall disproportionately to some. Sometimes by this we mean the costs to parents of their own time and money, and the opportunity costs of parenting. But for working parents, we may also mean the costs of private childcare provision. When a childcare system doesn't work as it should,

> Children [lose] out on vital early education and families remain trapped in poverty because they cannot make work pay. Childcare providers struggle with debts. Women fail to return to the labour market after they have children and the economy loses their skills and their taxes. The state faces greater welfare bills and high administrative costs for delivering a complex support system. (Rutter and Stocker, 2014, p 3)

Here, questions of gender roles clearly intersect with questions of distribution.

Meanwhile, there are also clear elements of recognition at stake. A male breadwinner model, for example, is a cultural vehicle as much as it is an economic template. It embodies assumptions about gender roles that penetrate wide swathes of social relations and dynamics, and do plenty of the heavy lifting when it comes to maintaining those relations in ways that disproportionately disadvantage women. Similarly, an assumption that care is a woman's responsibility, or that women should feel 'grateful' for partner involvement in domestic work, is not a distributed resource – at least not in a simple way. We might see this as a perception that helps facilitate, affirm and legitimise maldistribution. We might also see it as a *mis*perception that distorts and undervalues a form of practice. If being a 'housewife', for example, is regarded as being a lower-status role than professional roles of equivalent levels of difficulty or responsibility, this will have effects on the level of respect that 'housewives' experience in their everyday lives. To use Axel Honneth's phrase, this 'is injurious because it impairs these persons in their positive understanding of self – an understanding acquired by intersubjective means' (Honneth, 1992, p 89).

But the family economy works in other generational directions too, not least because families remain the primary site of care for older people. In 2015, Carers UK put the economic value of the contribution made by such unpaid carers in the UK at £132 billion per year – this being the cost of replacing that care with home care support, were a family member no longer available to carry out the role. This figure is almost double that of 2001, and very close to the total annual cost of health spending in the UK – £134.1 billion in 2014-15 (Carers UK, 2015). The patterns of social presumption work differently in the case of care 'upwards' from grown-up children to their parents. 'Family values' have a looser connotation here. Our definition of the family above has nothing to say about kids caring for their parents. The sociologist Talcott Parsons – prime exponent of the function-based definition – identified two functions in the family that are 'basic and irreducible': 'the primary socialisation of the children so that they can truly become members of the society into which they have been born', and 'the stabilisation of the adult personalities of the population of the society' (Parsons, 1956, p 16). Caring for a parent is not key to that second function: '[i]t is of course not uncommon to find a surviving parent of one or the other spouse ... but this is both statistically secondary, and it is clearly not felt to be the "normal" arrangement' (Parsons, 1956, p 10). There is less of an expectation that adult family members will have this or that kind of relationship, or indeed live near each other. The rules here seem different.

Yet such caring is still gendered. Of the 6.5 million unpaid carers identified in the 2011 UK census, 58% (3.34 million) were women (ONS, 2011a). One in four women aged 50-64 has caring responsibilities for older or disabled family members (Carers UK, 2015). With cuts to social care services in the aftermath of the 2008 financial crisis, caring of this kind has become increasingly politicised as an issue. The presumption that care will default to the family may bite particularly hard on working women, for example balancing part-time work with caring responsibilities in a package that adds up to considerably more than the average working week. The 2011 UK census identified 175,000 young carers – those under 18 who provide regular care to a family member who is physically or mentally ill, disabled or misusing drugs or alcohol (ONS, 2011a). Here we find ourselves especially far from the cartoon image of the nuclear family – and from Parsons' account of the family's chief functions.

The phenomenon of children and young people in caring roles provokes a media response that is itself revealing. On the one hand, we find a sense of shock and crisis. A *Daily Mail* headline tells of 'Thousands of young carers being robbed of childhood', above a story recounting the 'heartrending plight' of an 'army of children as young as five' who are being 'forced to care for disabled parents' (Clark, 2007). The assumption here – backed up by evidence of some young carers developing their own mental health problems, and being led to self-harm – is that there is something problematic or risky about the very scenario of a child missing out on childhood by taking on domestic responsibilities beyond their years – by being 'parentified' ahead of their time. The loss is typically counted in terms of time and experiences. So young carers are seen as losing out on friendships, on 'hanging out', on school engagement – and will feel different and sometimes stigmatised (Cass, 2007; O'Dell at al, 2010).

On the other hand, we find stories of heroism. For Young Carers Awareness Day in January 2016, the *Daily Express* featured interviews with 'three inspirational youngsters who go the extra mile for their families' (McCann, 2016). All three – all girls – talk of rewards as well as clear burdens and difficult situations, and are keen not to paint themselves as tragic victims. This pushes back against the rhetoric of loss and burden, and highlights dangers in adopting only that lens. For it allows for the possibility that young carers may find positive experiences – perhaps, unique benefits – in the very role that others perceive as a plight. There are particular rewards in being recognised as a carer – having one's experiences acknowledged, being allocated a social role, connecting with others in a similar position (Clarke and O'Dell, 2014, p 78).

The *Express* story reinforces the notion that care remains typically associated with women and girls: naturalised, as a definitively feminine capacity. While society talks more often and more positively about the nature of domestic work, and its impact on family members' lives, there are stubborn assumptions that caring comes naturally, is something that some people are just good at, is part and parcel of what families do, or is a domestic matter rather than a public one. Care talk is bound up with gender, and its place in the internal structures of families and the ways in which roles are allocated within them. But it is also – for all the tendency to view it as an aspect of personal choice, of intimacy, or individuals' navigation of their private lives – a public matter. Indeed its very framing as private may serve to 'undermine "public" arguments for increased support for shared responsibility both in the home and the community' (Lanning et al, 2013, p 5). Everyday domestic arrangements are inextricably connected to the wider landscape of questions about social justice. A specific set of such questions attach to the relationship between care and justice itself.

Justice and care

The need for care – of particular, long-term kinds – is part of the human condition. To put it another way, receiving adequate care is a condition of our survival and ability to flourish, as children and adults. We begin life exceptionally vulnerable, and take considerably longer than other animals to mature. Thus the issues just mentioned about the social place of care are not peripheral, but at the core of any discussion about what it takes for human life to go well. Whether we survive infancy, learn a language, develop confidence in our relations with others, fulfil this or that potential, become an adult with a secure identity – all of these are contingent on how we are treated in our early years. Because we are vulnerable, we are also, among species, especially dependent on others. This dependency is starkest among children and older people. But as Alasdair MacIntyre puts it, 'between these first and last stages our lives are characteristically marked by longer or shorter periods of injury, illness or other disablement and some among us are disabled for their entire lives' (MacIntyre, 1999, p 1). These are not culturally contingent aspects of our existence, or something we can opt out of, through personal preference. They are just how it goes. There is just no escaping dependency.

Approached from some angles, these might seem bland, if not boring points to make. But in the context of an exploration of issues concerning families and social justice, they take on a different kind of charge. It's one thing to say that human beings are often dependants, and that dependants need care. It's another thing to identify how much that requirement *matters*, compared with other aspects of human life, and other things we have reason to value. And it's another thing again to settle, socially, how we *meet* that requirement.

How much does dependency matter? We have to note here that for different reasons, theorists of social justice are wary even of identifying factors that somehow define the human condition, let alone attaching weight to those factors. Sometimes this is because of wariness about ethnocentrism – or the kinds of cultural imperialism risked when talking about 'humankind' from within one language, historical context or set of social conventions. In other words, it's easy to see how we could mistake features of life around here, in the early 21st century, for what life must be like in general, everywhere, forever. The assumption that we know what's important to other people's lives can become oppressive, however generously it is intended. So there is every reason to hesitate before speaking for the species as a whole (see Calder, 2007, ch 3). Sometimes the wariness comes from another direction. From one angle – and some libertarians do take this view – it is simply up to individuals themselves to determine the value of this or that aspect of their own lives. My priorities, or life projects, or conception of the 'good life', or what count as 'the basics' of my particular version of a human life, should be for me to decide – and not taken as pre-ordained according to some grand scheme of what's good for human beings.

This view is hard to sustain, just because some aspects of a human life – for example, our survival beyond infancy, a basic level of health and education – seem so clearly to be preconditions of us even coming to make choices at all, about what kind of life we would prefer to lead. Thus Rawls, for example, is happy to affirm a list of *primary goods* – the things we all want, whatever else we want, and whatever our 'plan of life' (Rawls, 1999, pp 54-55, 78-81). But any such list will always be contentious – and Rawls's is no exception (see, for example, Sen, 1995). Strikingly, this list happens not to include dependency-related goods – and seems (again) to assume an already-mature, rational adult without considering what goods may need to be in place for this achievement to take place. Comparing the relative priority of our being cared for with other goods, such us having the vote, or being able to express our views in public, is a contested business.

And then there's the question of how, if we do agree that care is primary, we meet that requirement. We have already seen something of the tissue of different factors and concerns arising here. Caring for dependants has been gendered and privatised. This reflects structural arrangements and cultural perceptions that are subject to change. Thinking about social justice requires that we think about whether and how those changes should happen. This means raising questions, not about whether human beings are vulnerable or dependent, but about what difference that makes to the kind of society we think is justifiable, fair or desirable. Eva Kittay sums up a general agenda:

> Questions of who takes on the responsibility of care, who does the hands-on care, who sees to it that the caring is done and done well, and who provides the support for the relationship of care and for both parties to the caring relationship – these are social and political questions. They are questions of social responsibility

and political will. How these questions are answered will determine whether the facts of human dependency can be made compatible with the full equality of all citizens – that is, whether full citizenship can be extended to all. (Kittay, 1999, p 1)

We have already had clear sight of why these questions press hard when our focus is on the family and social justice. But for Kittay – who, along with others such as Joan Tronto, Virginia Held and Carol Gilligan has been prominent in the delineation of a distinct 'ethics of care' – there are stakes here at another level.

Those stakes concern the relationship of care, itself, to justice, itself – that is to say whether the language of 'care' is part of the language of justice, or whether the two are conceptually quite distinct. To see what's at issue here, it helps to begin with the work of Carol Gilligan (1982, 1986). For Gilligan, 'justice' and 'care' represent two different kinds of sensibility, or 'voice', via which we might address morality. Justice is concerned with rights, impartiality, universality, respect for common humanity – a corollary of the liberal conception of a public sphere, populated by strangers, each to be treated with equal respect, their interests weighed disinterestedly. Here, the moral voice issues from the stance of a neutral referee, objectively weighing competing priorities or claims, and seeking to determine the right, or best outcome. So as a sensibility, justice involves standing back from the situation, and addressing it from the point of view of general principles. Care, on the other hand, entails a kind of immersion in the situation, and addressing it on its own terms. It attends to the particular, the contextual, to relationships, to nuances, to the individual needs of those involved – to responsibilities towards others, rather than to rights. Instead of learning principles, an ethic of care requires the development of a certain kind of orientation towards complex situations.

For Gilligan, controversially, these two voices are 'fundamentally incompatible' (1986, p 238). And more controversially still, they are stereotypically masculine and feminine. Confronted with an ethical dilemma, for example, women tend to reason in a different voice from men – focusing on the relationships at stake, mediating between different perspectives, identifying the specific needs at stake and seeking ways of addressing each of them. Importantly, for those interested in the ethical importance of care, these two claims are not part of the dress code. Indeed, many of those who have focused most and longest on the issues raised by care in relation to justice – such as Kittay and Tronto – have argued against Gilligan's dualism. Kittay, for example, has explored at close range the very relationship between the value of equality (which sits on the side of 'justice' if a distinction must be made) and the moral significance of dependency (ostensibly on the side of 'care'). She suggests that the two are best brought into dialectical relation, rather than addressed in separation (Kittay, 1999). Tronto, too, has stressed the importance of addressing the political and institutional context in which our consideration of human activities of care inevitably unfold, and keeping a simultaneous critical hold on both (1994, 2010).

Their cases are forceful, and significant in the context of the coverage of issues in this book, where there is no presumption that justice and care are fundamentally different kinds of voice. While there is not the space to argue at length the reasons for taking this stance, it's important to acknowledge it. In what follows, we will take it that the relational dynamics of care – its value for both receiver and giver – are a crucial element of social justice. A key contribution of the ethics of care has been to push dependency, and the texture of caring relationships, onto that agenda in a way that, for most of the historical unfolding of debates on social justice, it wasn't.

Children themselves

Children, too, have mostly been absent from the scene when political philosophers have done their thinking about the just society. Sometimes they feature at the margins. Mostly, though, the models at stake have tended to assume already-mature, rational adults as the participants in the realms of society that matter. An exception is Plato's *Republic*, dating from the 370s BC, and usually taken as the literary starting-point of western discussions of morality and social justice. It is also takes the rare position of recommending the eradication of the family – at least, for the rulers of an ideally just society. The upbringing of those children should be collectivised. The children themselves should be the result of sex taking place between 'men and women who are astoundingly good'. Officials will then take charge of them, and 'hand them over to nurses (who live in a separate section of the community)' (Plato, 1993, pp 173-4. Their upbringing will not be left to chance, or to parental whim, but tightly managed in expert, collective institutions.

Plato's plan has few exponents these days. We'd be surprised to find it setting the agenda for a radio phone-in discussion of family policy. Yet it raises two issues that remain fundamental to how we think about families and social justice. One is luck – the lottery of childhood. The children we are is a matter of biological luck, carried in the genes we happen to inherit. And the childhoods we have is a matter of sociological luck, located in the class position, beliefs, values and priorities of the parents or carers we happen to have. In neither case does it make coherent sense to say that children deserve their start in life. In both senses, life seems to start out, rather than *fairly* in any obvious way, with the chance dealing of a hand. The care we receive – the ways our early needs our met – is also a matter of luck (Gheaus, 2009). Plato's version of the collectivisation of child rearing would take much of the sting out of this. Children would be the product of arranged sex between selected members of society. And they would receive an upbringing based not on the happenstance views of one or two individuals, but on the best of current wisdom. The phrase 'life's not fair' would apply very differently in that kind of set-up, if it had purchase at all. And the other issue pushed forward by Plato's model is that, as we have seen, children are in important senses a public good. Society as a whole has very good reasons to care that child bearing takes place, and that child rearing happens in good ways. One generation has every reason to feel anxious about its relation to the next, and about how the next is faring – not least because children contribute to our future well-being (see Olsaretti, 2013). The maintenance of social structures – and there being society at all – depends on there being children who come in time to occupy certain roles, to grow up into taxpayers, and to care for older people.

A whole new arena opens up when we think about the well-being of children themselves – for example, whether they have rights, and what those rights might be. Here we find quite a basic set of questions about which 'common sense' gives decidedly mixed messages. How does the well-being of children compare with that of adults? And how should we perceive the relationship between these two states of being, in terms of our entitlements and how we should be treated? Are children best seen, in Patrick Tomlin's vivid imagery, as 'saplings' (incomplete versions of adults) or as 'caterpillars' – a fundamentally different kind of thing from an adult (Tomlin, 2016)? When, within the lifespan, are the best years of our lives – or is it even sensible to try to generalise about that at all? Article 3.1 of the United Nations Convention on the Rights of the Child (UNCRC) states this:

> In all actions concerning children, whether undertaken by public or private social welfare institutions, courts of law, administrative authorities of legislative bodies, the best interests of the child shall be a primary consideration. (United Nations, 1989)

But determining 'best interests' is, of course, a perilous business. Even if we are happy to affirm – as in the previous section – that there are shared basic needs and features of the human condition, this does not necessarily help with a discretionary judgement about what is best for this or that child, in this or that situation, or which among the different interests at stake should be given priority. Let us go back to our earlier list:

- ensuring that children have an adequately nutritious diet;
- ensuring that children are educated;
- the setting of an age of sexual consent;
- decisions about medical intervention, for example vaccination or organ transplant;
- the appropriateness of smacking or other corporal punishment;

- the adoption of a particular set of religious beliefs.

Here we can see how discussions of what is in a child's best interests will be complicated by the dimensions of their situation, and the particular factors at stake. Again, matters seem less controversial near the top of the list. But debates about smacking centre precisely on differences in points of view – sometimes vehement ones – as to what is in a child's best interest. Moreover, who is in the best position to determine this in any one case? A parent, because they know the child best, or love them? Children themselves? Experts on child development? The state, because it is in the best position to enact general, consistent rules? It is one thing to identify basic areas of potential harm to a child's best interests – lack of nutrition, neglect, abuse – and to prioritise these in determining a standard of satisfactory treatment. It seems quite another to feel entirely confident that we can determine what is best for children.

The UNCRC's explicit aim is to address children as 'human beings with a distinct set of rights instead of as passive objects of care and charity' (United Nations, 1989). According to Article 12,

> States Parties shall assure to the child who is capable of forming his or her own views the right to express those views freely in all matters affecting the child, the views of the child being given due weight in accordance with the age and maturity of the child. (United Nations, 1989)

This aim is cast in complex light when we consider the pre-eminence of the family in mediating the life of the child. Were children raised in collectivised institutions, we can see how this right might be managed and honoured. There could then be procedural provision to ensure that every child capable of forming and voicing their views on matters affecting them was duly heard. Across family units, there can be no such provision. In the 1990s era of the Australian soap opera *Neighbours*, the Kennedy family (mother Susan, a teacher; father Karl, a general practitioner; and their children Malcolm, Libby and Billy) used to hold periodic family conferences, in the manner of a democratic staff meeting. This was depicted as a middle-class affectation. In any case, it's neither standard practice across domestic set-ups where children reside, nor something that is ever likely to be. Those set-ups are radically inconsistent.

This poses a barrier to the realisation of the assumption that 'children are rights holders with an entitlement to participate in decisions on matters which affect them' (Butler and Drakeford, 2013, p 18). The impact of all rights is limited by the scope for their actual take-up. In the case of children's rights, the gap between legislation and take-up is made bigger by the intervening influences that families wield. They do not, by themselves, stop children being subjected to unkindness, to distant indifference, to the lack of attention or eye contact, to coldness, and other common enough features of mundane domestic relationships that may have all kinds of short- and long-term impacts on the quality and direction of children's lives. Indeed, rights may matter most in situations where family relationships have broken down, rather than when they are (however imperfectly) stable (Noggle, 2017).

Parental partiality

The influence of parents is key to our final theme. Because it recurs later, we will do no more than introduce it here. The issue goes like this. We assume we have a right to be partial towards family members. Parents, especially, assume that they are justified, perhaps obliged, to prioritise the interests of their children over other children, or other people in general. They may assume this even where acting this way seems to confer unfair benefits – and generates substantial inequalities between the children concerned. The right to raise one's children seems just *inevitably* to involve this kind of preferential treatment. The fact that parents (or indeed grandparents) treat their kids preferentially is part of what makes them *parents* (or indeed grandparents), rather than some other kind of relation. I buy my son but not yours a scooter for his birthday, because he's *my* son and buying the same thing for *your* son would seem random, or (for example if our sons were friends) like muscling in, showing off, or some kind of mistake in manners. And not buying a scooter for a stranger of the same age, perhaps abroad, perhaps more needy than my own, does not seem like a dereliction of duty. Doing so may seem – again – random or arbitrary as a gesture.

This works so far, in terms of chiming with most people's intuitions. But issues of parental partiality really kick in when we're discussing not buying scooters, but decisions with bigger impacts. Nobody thinks parents can do *anything* to benefit their kids. So there is some kind of line around what Brighouse and Swift call 'legitimate parental partiality' (Brighouse and Swift, 2009). A simple example of Swift's conveys the need for such a line:

> An American woman was charged with attempted murder, accused of trying to kill a girl who was competing with her daughter for a place as a cheerleader. That mother showed excessive concern for her daughter's interests. She went too far. Most evenings, I read a bedtime story to my kids. I am showing a special, partial interests in my children. I know that reading to them gives them advantages that will help them in the future, advantages not enjoyed by less fortunate others. It is unfair that they don't get what mine do. The playing field is not level; our bedtime stories tilt it in their favour. Even so, few would advocate that they be banned. Bedtime stories are the right side of the line. (Swift, 2003, p 9)

Swift uses this example in a book about school choices – an obvious way in which parents' decisions may or may not be crossing that line into illegitimate parental partiality. Well, I say obvious. For some, choosing how you educate your child – whether, for example, to send them to a fee-paying school – is a staple part of the parenting brief. There is no case to answer. Yet *somewhere* on the scale from murder to bedtime stories, we pass the point where parental partiality becomes acceptable. Here's a possible version of that scale:

• murdering rivals;

- paying for private education;
- bequeathing property;
- bequeathing money;
- arranging internships via personal contacts;
- paying for extra tuition to help with school tests;
- helping with homework;
- discussing current affairs at mealtimes;
- paying for dance lessons;
- paying for driving lessons;
- arranging cinema trips;
- reading bedtime stories.

Is that scale in the right order, in terms either of degree of impact or permissibility? This is hotly debatable, just because there are so many different ways of conferring advantage on your children. But all of these are clearly ways – in a world where not all children get the same – of advantaging your own children over others. When does that advantage become unfair? And when is it parents' *fault* that it's unfair?

Conclusion: the family in public

The job of this chapter has been to set out some of the ways in which families raise questions about social justice, or, to put it another way, some of the ways in which practices and values (often the most routine kind) associated with family life connect up, and sometimes seemingly conflict, with wider questions about fairness and the principles by which we would like society as a whole to be governed. It is partly because family life is so important, and because it is so strongly valued by so many, that these questions are important. But as we have seen, recognising this gives us few answers about what exactly is valuable about family life, or what is permissible in the name of family, or what family members are entitled to do for each other. One thing it is vital to stress again, in closing, is that 'family' is not simply, or even mostly, a private matter. No family is an island. Having and rearing children has public consequences, and already reflects, channels and reinforces existing public circumstances. One of the many things problematic about Margaret Thatcher's famous statement to *Woman's Own* magazine – 'There's no such thing as society. There are individual men and women and there are families' (Thatcher, 1987) – is its implied denial of the tangled interrelationships among families, and between families and other institutions. As we'll see, the ways in which these relationships unfold are, to a large degree, what we mean when we talk about social mobility.

THREE

Social mobility and class fate

Few things are as ripe for 'proof' by anecdotal evidence as social mobility. It's like a special kind of magnet for folk wisdom. And the sense that it is stalling or in retreat raises familiar forms of qualm. Such qualms are often expressed in terms of a projection of one's own story onto others.

Mobility stories

Here's composer, artist and ex-member of Roxy Music Brian Eno in March 2016:

> Social mobility has slipped back. If I were 20 now I'd have so much less opportunity than I did. A-stars and the right university have become very important, and nearly all those things eventually come down to money. (Eno, 2016, p 17)

Here's an example from a *Sunday Times* story in July 2015:

> Georgina Jones, 26, who grew up in a council estate in Peckham, southeast London, found her career prospects were transformed when she was given an internship at 16 by the Social Mobility Foundation. She now works as an associate at Taylor Wessing, a law firm, and, although she believes she would have made it this far because of her personal drive, it is time to increase the support offered to others to convert early promise into later success. (Hellen, 2015, p 5)

And here's BBC broadcaster Andrew Neil, from a little further back:

> I ... was brought up in a council house.... I made it to an elite
> 16th Century grammar school in Paisley and then Glasgow
> University, a world-class 15th Century institution. I was part of
> the post-World War II meritocracy that slowly began to infiltrate
> the citadels of power, compete head-to-head against those with
> the 'right' background and connections and – more often than
> not – win. Britain's class system seemed to be changing. (Neil,
> 2011)

These perspectives are those of people who have 'made it'. Jones
believes she would have made it anyway. The (as it happens, privately
educated) Eno thinks the life chances of people like him are worse
now. Neil is convinced that it was grammar schools that gave kids
like him a 'leg up'. Each speaks with sincere confidence about how
their story would have gone, had things been different. This isn't an
exceptional trait of the successful. Most of us (he says, anecdotally)
have running explanations in our heads about the balance between
luck, talent, grit and circumstance in how we got to wherever we are
on the 'social ladder'.

Projections of a sweeping claim across a section of the population
are often what people remember. They stick. In 2008, Dame Carol
Black, former National Director for Health and Work, said this:

> We have got places where there are three generations of men
> who have never worked. If your grandfather never worked and
> your father never worked, why would you think work is the
> normal thing to do? I think it is an awful thing to inflict on a
> child. I worry about what this does to the fabric of our society,
> let alone the economy. (Cited in Koster, 2008)

Reporting this, the *Daily Mail* made the following claim on the back
of it: 'Thousands of children are growing up in families where their
parents and grandparents have never worked' (Koster, 2008). Speaking

at the Centre for Social Justice in 2009, Iain Duncan Smith, later Secretary of State for Work and Pensions, repeated the claim: '... on some deprived estates ... often *three generations of the same family have never worked*' (cited in MacDonald, 2015, emphasis in original). And in 2011, the then Secretary of State for Work and Pensions Chris Grayling cranked it up another notch on the BBC's *Newsnight* programme: '... there are *four generations* of families where no-one has ever had a job' (cited in Hern, 2012).

This claim is about how a particular symptom of inequality runs in families. A culture of worklessness is inflicted on children, like a kind of assault on their life chances. Dame Carol's own story puts this in context:

> We really weren't wealthy – on our bookshelf we had the Bible and a full set of Dickens, and that was it – but my father had a job at the Co-op and a secure wage, and I knew how important that was.... There was structure and there was order, and I think that is what is lacking now in a lot of families. If you don't have to get up for work in the morning, why get up? (Cited in Donnelly, 2008)

This fits readily within a well-established framing of the relationship between domestic circumstances and attitudes to work, epitomised in Chancellor George Osborne's announcement of benefits cuts in 2012, with its identification of 'shirkers' and 'strivers':

> Where is the fairness, we ask, for the shift-worker, leaving home in the dark hours of the early morning, who looks up at the closed blinds of their next-door neighbour sleeping off a life on benefits? (Cited in Channel 4 News, 2012)

These shirkers, says the grander narrative, have been bred that way. The inheritance of a culture of blinds-closed inertia helps make swathes of people decide never to work. The welfare system must be redesigned to break this cycle, rather than (as previously) reinforcing it, across three or four generations. So it is that a narrative becomes fixed and nailed down.

Except that as it turns out, the 'generations' story is a myth. A 2012 study for the Joseph Rowntree Foundation (Shildrick, 2012) set out to find out whether long-term unemployment might be explained through 'cultures of worklessness'. Researchers in Glasgow and Middlesbrough, using every tool at their disposal to locate families with three generations that had never worked, in areas with among the highest levels of long-term unemployment, found not a single one. *Not a single family.* Less than 1% of households have two generations who have never worked – a 2011 study placed the figure at 0.1% (Macmillan, 2011; Full Fact, 2012). If there are any with three, 'they can only account for a miniscule fraction of workless people'. What the researchers found, instead, were parents who wanted their kids to get jobs, and young adults keen to avoid 'the poverty, worklessness and other problems experienced by their parents' (MacDonald and Shildrick, 2012).

So even the most familiar social mobility stories are not, well, the whole story. Sometimes they are downright misleading. But those stories do a lot of work. One reason for this is that social mobility, as Lynsey Hanley observes, 'is presented as both the central problem of class inequality and its solution' (Hanley, 2016, p 136). It is the absence of it that hits headlines, and makes it seem a catch-all remedy. As mentioned in the Preface, some (like former Labour prime minister Gordon Brown) will talk as if social mobility is the new social justice. If only we had social mobility, class inequality wouldn't exist, or at least, not in its more pernicious versions. Thus Alan Milburn, Chair of the Social Mobility Commission, identifies higher social mobility – reducing the extent to which a person's class or income is dependent on the class or income of their parents – as 'the new holy grail of public policy', bought into across the political spectrum (Milburn, 2015). So there's a discussion to be had as to whether social mobility is indeed the ultimate answer. To do that, means identifying what exactly it might be the answer *to*.

The shape of class fate

I'm using 'class fate' as a shorthand term for intergenerational inequality, or social immobility. Class fate is the tendency for people's ultimate class position or income level to replicate that of their parents. It reflects, on one level, a lack of what is termed *absolute* (or intergenerational) social mobility. Absolute mobility reflects the class or income position of an adult compared with that of their parents. So the more children of unskilled workers who are lawyers, the more absolute upward mobility there is. But the contours of class fate can also be seen in measures of *relative* (or intragenerational) mobility. Relative mobility compares how different groups in society are faring, relative to each other. So if we compare, within a generation, how the children of unskilled workers and lawyers fare in terms of class and income, we are looking at relative mobility. It's a matter of comparing how many who start lower down move up (upward mobility), compared with how many who start higher up fall down (downward mobility) or stay put (stability). An example from Richard Breen helps bring out the different implications of each:

> Suppose that my father was a clerk and that I am a manager: then, in absolute terms I have been upwardly mobile. But suppose that, in my father's generation, being a clerk gave him a class position that was better than half the population, whereas, in my generation, being a manager puts me in a class position which is better than, say, 40 per cent of the population. Then in relative terms I have been downwardly mobile because my rank is worse than my father's: half of the population were in a better position than him whereas 60 per cent are in a better class position than me, and this is so even though I have an objectively better class position than he had. (Breen, 2010, pp 417-18)

Importantly, as this example shows, it is possible for high levels of absolute mobility to coincide with low levels of relative mobility. Everyone's kids might tend to be better off than their parents, at the same time as gaps between the incomes of those born poorer and those born richer are preserved.

Of necessity, looking at the big picture of trends in social mobility, these ups and downs will be gauged according to broad categories. Class schemas come in various kinds – a recent, valuably multidimensional version emerging from the work of Mike Savage and a team of fellow sociologists at the London School of Economics, based on their Great British Class Survey, run through the BBC. This schema identifies seven classes, arranged according to their relative degrees not just of economic capital (levels of income, wealth and property), but also social capital (social connections and networks) and cultural capital (tastes, interests and orientations). So in principle, these three – the distinction stems from the sociological theory of Pierre Bourdieu (see, for example, Bourdieu, 1997) – may operate separately from one another. One can be culture-rich (well educated, *au fait* with contemporary art, knowing the 'right' ways to speak) but economically poor. Or economically well-off but poorly connected (having few friends in high places, or with useful skills). Each of these is a kind of *capital*, because it provides a source of leverage – of advantages over other people. This matters, as we'll see.

But historically, the richest analysis of social mobility has come in terms of a class model based on occupation. Here, the benchmark is John Goldthorpe's seven-class schema, running from higher-grade professionals and company directors (class I) to semi- and unskilled manual and agricultural workers (class VII) (Goldthorpe et al, 1987, pp 40-3). He reduces this to a simplified three-point hierarchy, which has since served, with some variations, as the sociological basis for mobility analysis. It looks at movement between what has come to be called a salariat (classes I and II), an intermediate grouping (classes III, IV and sometimes V) and a working class (classes VI and VII, and sometimes also V).

So the quick story of post-war social mobility – the 'golden age' of absolute mobility – can be told succinctly as a doubling in size of the salariat between 1939 and the early 1970s from 20% to 40% of the male labour market, so that men entering the labour market were now equally likely to be entering the salariat as the working class. There were similar upward trends for women, albeit extending less into the salariat, and more into the intermediate classes (Mandler, 2016).

What's crucial here is that it's primarily the *labour market* doing the work: many of these salariat positions required no formal qualifications at all, and only a small proportion were graduate professions. (A university degree was not required to enter law or accountancy, for example, until the 1970s.) And the trends reflect a steady expansion of the service sector, and 'in particular in professional employment across education, health and other parts of the welfare state' (Boliver and Byrne, 2013, p. 51). These trends are widely taken to have slowed, partly because there is now less 'room at the top' – less expansion in the upper echelons of the employment structure, and more at the bottom. As Goldthorpe observes, 'Young people entering the labour market today face far less favourable mobility prospects than did their parents – or their grandparents' (Goldthorpe, 2016, p 36). The age, if ever it was, is no longer golden. Mobility in the UK has slowed drastically – to among the lowest levels in the world. So it is that by 2010, in the UK, a person's earnings were more likely to echo their father's than in any other country (OECD, 2010).

Does this broad picture pick up the finer dynamics of class gradations, as deployed by Savage and colleagues? Well, not really. What we find are prompts for further analysis, rather than intimate dissections of the different currents of cause and effect that go into cementing class fate. Those prompts are usually best conveyed in tables or diagrams. Elements of the UK story since 1970 can be captured in this way. Table 3.1 gives a picture of absolute social mobility, in terms of income, for those born in 1970, compared with those born in 1958. It's important here that each shows class fate in what Robert D. Putnam terms a 'rearview mirror' (Putnam, 2015, p 44). Because class fate 'plays out over entire generations' (Clark, 2014, p 159), and because the best way to get a handle on its patterns are by comparing (say) a daughter's income or class position in mid-life with their parents' income or class position in mid-life, any numbers we latch onto are a 'lagging indicator'. They're delayed stories of previous decades, rather than a simple snapshot of now. But if we want numbers, such are the indicators we must go by.

Table 3.1: The link between parental and child income for those born in 1958 and 1970

Income mobility for children of parents in the poorest quartile (per cent)		
Year birth of child	1958	1970
Chances of staying in poorest quartile	31	38
Chances of moving to richest quartile	17	16
Income mobility for children of parents in the richest quartile (per cent)		
Year birth of child	1958	1970
Chances of staying in richest quartile	35	38
Chances of moving to poorest quartile	17	11

Source: Willetts (2011), based on Machin et al (2005).

So adults are now more likely to have a higher income if their parents have, or had, a higher income, or, the other way around: the kids of the richest parents are now more strongly insured against downward income mobility. And the kids of the poorest parents are less likely to move up. The link between parent and child income is strengthening over time.

Table 3.2 shows that UK adults are more likely to have a higher-status (and, usually, higher-paid) job if their parents have, or had, a higher income. Here, there are fluctuations: not all of these figures are rising decade on decade. But they are so very stark, that this seems small consolation. These numbers need to be set against the fact that 7% of children attend independent schools.

Who knew private education was the key to pop success? Table 3.2 shows that Brian Eno is entirely right to be concerned about social mobility slipping back. But not for future Brian Enos. Those 'making it' in music (here we're talking about UK artists who had a top 40 album between 2011 and 2014) are now three times more likely than

Table 3.2: Percentage of members of elite and professional occupations attending independent schools

Category of the elite	Proportion attending independent school
Senior judges	71%
Senior armed forces officers	62%
Commons Select Committee chairs	57%
Diplomats	53%
Lords	50%
Members of Sunday Times Rich List	44%
TV, film and music industry figures	44%
Newspaper columnists	43%
Radio 4 influential women	42%
Cabinet ministers	36%
Rugby Union players – England, Scotland and Wales	35%
MPs	33%
Chief constables/Police and Crime Commissioners	22%
Pop stars	22%
University vice-chancellors	20%
Local government leaders	15%

Source: Social Mobility and Child Poverty Commission (2015a)

the general population to have attended a fee-paying school. Savage and colleagues' analysis of the Great British Class Survey found the elite class to be far more difficult to enter than any of the other social classes. Average incomes are highest in those jobs where the workforce is most likely to have been recruited from the most privileged families. And 'stable members of the elite tend to have higher levels of all three type of capital than those who have recently gained entry to this group' (Savage et al, 2015, p 208). Even within the elite, it's those coming from the most privileged backgrounds who come out on top.

Figure 3.1: The Great Gatsby curve

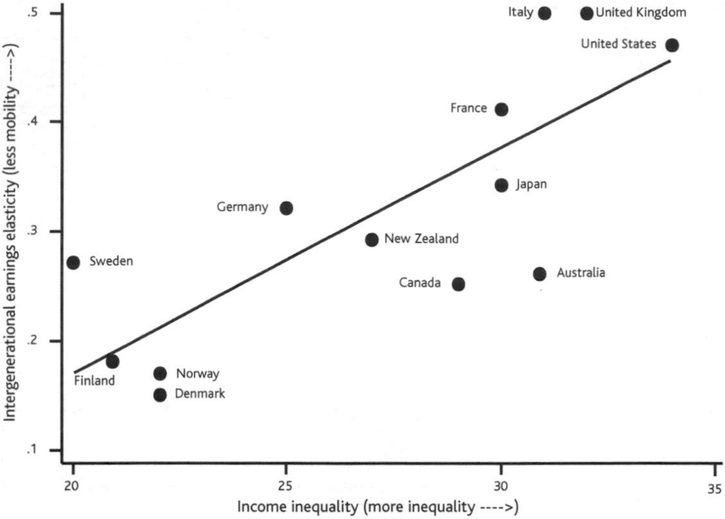

Source: Corak (2013)

Figure 3.1 shows, in short, that 'in countries where income is more unequally spread, the next generation enjoys less mobility' (Clark, 2014, p 159). Moving horizontally from left to right represents a movement from low inequality to high inequality, as the Gini coefficient rises. Moving vertically from bottom to top (where 'elasticity' refers to the strength of the link between what a parent earns and what their child goes on to earn) represents a movement from more mobility in economic status across generations to less economic mobility (Corak, 2012). The picture isn't uniform: it suggests that while Australia is very nearly as unequal in income terms as the UK, it enjoys higher levels of mobility. But like the previous two – and like the wealth of analysis in Richard Wilkinson and Kate Pickett's widely influential study *The spirit level* (Wilkinson and Pickett, 2010) – it shows that the UK has a big class fate problem. What it adds to the mix is that the UK has an *especially* big class fate problem. And as Kitty Stewart says, it 'lends support to the hypothesis that boosting mobility will be harder where inequality is higher' (Stewart, 2016, p 105).

These three depictions of class fate are not, of course, the complete story. They are snippets and panoramic views. They don't pick up the finer mechanisms at play. Neither do they tell us about the human textures of the lives at stake. They don't show what goes on in the households of those who find that their ultimate destination in life is, in early 21st-century Britain, startlingly predictable. They don't say much about those who buck the trends – senior judges, for example, who elbow their way in from a non-privately educated background – or why that bucking happens. (Georgina Jones believes that circumstances are still fair *enough* for her own attributes to have overcome barriers that might have thwarted others – though we can presume from these numbers that she needed a good deal more by way of exceptional personal qualities to succeed in law than many of her colleagues will have.) And they don't tell us what factors, among those contributing, weigh most heavily in causing these overall figures. There are three obvious factors to consider. The first is the one that grammar school boy Andrew Neil assumes to be crucial – education.

Is class fate education's fault?

> Working class children must be taught to think and act like the middle classes if they are to get into the best universities and top professions, a Government adviser has said. (Graham, 2014)

Neil's stance on grammar schools is a common one. It is echoed in the spirit of the words of the government adviser quoted here – but also, more literally, in a UK Independence Party (UKIP) policy promulgated in the Welsh Assembly elections in May 2015: to reintroduce grammar schools, accessible via selection by exam at ages 12, 13 or 16, with a minimum 10% intake of pupils from low-income backgrounds. The policy's stated aim is to 'celebrate' differences in ability and rate of learning 'by giving pupils the chance to mould their studies to fit the skills and ambitions unique to them' (Gill, 2016). Framed in terms of social mobility, the case for grammar schools typically goes like this:

- Premise 1: there are differences of educational ability across the social classes.
- Premise 2: selective education provides the optimal way of allowing the most academic to succeed, whatever their class background.
- Conclusion: state-provided selective education is key to maximising the extent to which access to higher-paid or elite professions is determined on merit, rather than class background.

Each element could be explored at far greater length than space here allows. Let's take the first as read. Even those who reject the assumption that rather than innate intelligence it's class barriers that are crucial to holding back non-high achievers (see, for example, Saunders, 1996, 2010) would concede that *however* abilities are distributed among the social classes, each contains a mixture. And so educational opportunities might be distributed in better or worse ways, to allow children and young people from across the class spectrum to achieve their potential. It's really premise 2 that is the pivot of the case.

But premise 2 doesn't hold up in the way presumed in the stances of Neil and UKIP. Or rather, the evidence for it can't be found where people usually look for it. A routine move – Neil makes it – is to assume that the post-war 'golden age' of social mobility was achieved on the back of the period, up to the late 1960s, when grammar schools cohabited with secondary moderns, and maximum meritocracy was achieved. Meritocracy is, in this sense, the reverse of intergenerational privilege. Those rising rise on the basis of their abilities (intelligence, talent, effort) and actual achievements, rather than inherited status. If the ideal is a world where social positions reflect only merit (a far bigger 'if' than political consensus suggests, as we'll get back to later), impediments to this constitute unfair, inefficient discrimination. Neil's assumption – with his own story as back-up – is that grammar schools were a vital engine of meritocracy. In David Kynaston's history of

Britain from 1957-62, we find the figure of the 'classic meritocrat' – a member of 'Britain's New Class', armed, as Frank Hilton put it, with 'their intelligence, their energy, and too much choice'. The archetype would pass 'the triple historical test of (a) born in 1933 or later (b) being working-class and (c) going to grammar school' (Kynaston, 2015, p 207). For grammar school fans, this figure is emblematic: the personification of the golden age, 'advancing largely by dint of their own endeavours, as opposed to socio-economic background and connection' (Kynaston, 2015, p 203).

But if there were 'classic meritocrats', it's not at all clear that what 'made' them was the grammar school. We have already seen why. The transitions into and out of that 'golden age' were driven primarily not by changes in the education system, but by changes in employment opportunities. Mobility was fuelled by the expansion of managerial and professional employment, of the amount of 'room at the top'. It was slowed again by changes in the class structure (Goldthorpe, 2016). If ex-grammar school kids were now occupying much more prominent roles in institutions, corporations and public life, that's largely because there were now a greater number of prominent roles in institutions, corporations and public life. 'More children from working-class families were swept up into the professions because the professions were hungrily swallowing up more and more people' (Bloodworth, 2016, p 45). Peter Mandler expands the point. In the 'golden age',

> the form that upward mobility took tended to bypass educational qualifications altogether. Women went straight into the intermediate classes at school-leaving age, into clerical and retail jobs that did not require educational qualifications of any kind. Men similarly moved into the intermediate classes at school-leaving age, acquired new skills and aspirations on the job, and were then available for recruitment into the salariat based on these life skills rather than their increasingly distant educational experience.... [W]ith the exception of the small numbers who had no secondary education at all, upward mobility in this period was experienced almost equally by people at all levels of

educational attainment. Even a university degree didn't really improve your chances of upward mobility very much, because if you got a university degree in this period you were likely to be from a salariat background already. (Mandler, 2016)

This is worth quoting at length not because grammar schooling is necessarily a burning policy issue (though there are currently moves afoot to re-ignite it), but because of the ubiquity of the insistence that 'grammar schools were the best leg up for the talented working class'. A case can be made that really, the era of grammar schools and secondary moderns operating in tandem, directing kids' lives one way or the other through selection on the basis of the 11-plus, left social mobility more or less where it was. The best leg up for the talented working class – in the most sustained period of upward mobility the UK has seen – was provided by prodigious expansion in the jobs market, amid the long post-war economic boom. To say that it was the grammar schools that did it is a bit (though admittedly, not entirely) like saying that grammar schools were the reason that England won the World Cup in 1966, and their retreat is the reason why they haven't progressed beyond the semi-finals of a major tournament since.

And it's again worth reinforcing the point that even when patterns of absolute upward mobility have been at their strongest, relative rates of class mobility have been remarkably constant, stretching right back to the period between the wars; that is, as Goldthorpe points out (referring mostly to the systems of England and Wales),

> ... over a period characterised by a series of major educational reforms, all carried through with some degree of egalitarian intent, including the introduction of secondary education for all following the Butler Act of 1944, the increase in the school leaving age to 15 in 1947 and to 16 in 1972, the move from the selective tripartite system of secondary education to comprehensive schools from the later 1960s, the replacement of O-levels by GCSEs in 1988, and two major waves of expansion

in tertiary education in the 1960s and 1990s. (Goldthorpe, 2012, p 18)

It has all made rather less difference than the grand ambitions of reforming education ministers might have one believe (see also Piketty, 2014, pp 484-6).

Does education then shrivel away, as a relevant factor in class fate? Do educational aims and expectations make no difference at all to relative mobility, as we slide towards a climate of 'deteriorating employment prospects in a deregulated labour market' (Ainley, 2016, p 61)? Is social mobility *simply* the plaything of larger, structural economic forces? Of course, this doesn't follow. Just because one particular strategy, in one historical period, seems not to have had the impact that many assume it to have had, this doesn't itself downgrade the impact of education in general on class fate. There is a strong plausibility about the idea that education is a crucial lever. If not, we wouldn't get so anxious about the relative opportunities of children attending private and state schools.

Like the New Labour regime before it, and whether or not in denial about Goldthorpe's analysis, the Social Mobility and Child Poverty Commission regards schools as 'the cornerstone of efforts to improve social mobility' (2015b, p vi). Since 2010, the rhetoric of UK governments (both coalition and then Conservative) has laid heavy emphasis on the regrettability of the gaps in future prospects between state- and privately educated children and in educational attainment in state schools between those entitled to free school meals and the rest. This has been echoed by the Welsh and Scottish governments. There is a shared sense of emergency about the kinds of evidence summed up in the graph with which Chapter One of this book begins: that the highest-attaining poorer kids fall behind the averagely attaining richer kids by the age of 16. And the assumption that what goes on in school matters is a natural corollary of the notion that family background is a major determinant of life chances. After all, schools, in principle, might work as an egalitarian counterbalance to the hierarchy of family backgrounds.

Various steps have been taken by governments to tackle the attainment gap, including the targeting of resources. The Westminster government announced a 'pupil premium' in 2010, allocating extra funding per capita for each pupil admitted from a low-income household (see Chowdry et al, 2010). In 2007 the Welsh government introduced a policy of free breakfasts, to ease the household budgets of the worse-off, help lay down good nutritional habits, aid concentration, promote sociability, make children more receptive to learning, and, by extending the school day, lessen the childcare burden (Butler and Drakeford, 2013, p 16). In Scotland since 2015, as in England since 2013, eligibility for free school meals at lunchtime has now been extended to all children in the first three years of primary school (Robinson, 2013). The stated aim, for the then-Deputy Prime Minister Nick Clegg, was to ensure that 'every child gets the chance they deserve'. While free school meals may benefit everyone, there is no direct evidence that these measures have reduced the attainment gap between richer and poorer children. Wales, for example, saw a general rise in attainment at GCSE level between 2008 and 2013 – for pupils eligible for free school meals, as well as those not. But the results for the better-off children rose by more than those of the worse-off (Equality and Human Rights Commission, 2015, p 11).

There's an important, resounding point here about relative mobility. Across time, and whatever the general social norm in terms of standards or expectations of qualifications, there is a remarkable propensity on the part of the already better-off to make more of whatever education is available. Those who arrive in state schools best equipped to exploit them – for example, those whose parents have university degrees – will profit most from any general advances. Parents' (and indeed grandparents') capital will allow better-off state educated kids to live in higher-priced housing near better schools, to get extra tuition, to pay postgraduate fees, and simply (in terms of cultural capital) to embolden their children to feel that the educational road is one down which they are expected and entitled to travel – a road *for them*. And in case that journey doesn't work out, better-off parents are more able to fund a safety net, or a plan B.

And of course, those attending private schools will segue more smoothly, on leaving education, into professional careers and find rising within them comes more readily, because private school is designed to advantage them in precisely those ways. That's what parents are paying for. Unfairness is part of their very *purpose*, as Alan Bennett barely needs to point out, but does so beautifully:

> [I]t is hard not to think that we all know that to educate not according to ability but according to the social situation of the parents is both wrong and a waste. Private education is not fair. Those who provide it know it. Those who pay for it know it. Those who have to sacrifice in order to purchase it know it. And those who receive it know it, or should. And if their education ends without it dawning on them then that education has been wasted. (Bennett, 2014)

If it's not fair, it's because of its dogged role in class fate – and because the greater the levels of inequality in a society, the greater the relative gains of privately educating one's children. This latter factor may form part of the explanation for Wilkinson and Pickett's finding that, among the eight rich countries for which relevant social mobility data is available, public expenditure on education is strongly linked to the degree of income inequality:

> In Norway, the most equal of the eight, almost all (97.8 per cent) spending on school education is public expenditure. In contrast, in the USA, the least equal of this group of countries, only about two-thirds (68.2 per cent) of the spending on school education is public money. (Wilkinson and Pickett, 2010, p 161)

Across the Nordic countries in general (Norway, Sweden, Finland and Denmark[1]), the numbers of children in fee-paying education are proportionately very small. All of those four are among the most equal in the world, in terms of levels of income.

And yet, 'education according to the social situation of parents' pervades the state system too, despite its purpose quite specifically *not* being to deliver unfairness. Any one intervention will seem like a blunt instrument. This is partly because the work done by inequality is already under way before school age. For the Social Mobility and Child Poverty Commission, recent 'efforts to improve the school-readiness of the poorest children are uncoordinated, confused and patchy' (Social Mobility and Child Poverty Commission, 2015b, p vi). Schools do not equalise economic capital (by reducing material inequalities) in any direct way, and are limited in what they might do to redistribute cultural capital – for example, in terms of the confidence of children to exploit school resources fully, or to see academic success as being 'for them', something we'll return to shortly.

Any education system will do its work against a backdrop of inequality that bites on families and children before and after they come through the school gates – and that helps in the girding of what sociologists of education call 'maximally maintained inequality': how educational inequalities 'stick' from one generation to the next (see, for example, Raftery and Hout, 1993). As Sonia Exley puts it:

> Without broader redistribution and political change outside the realm of education, formal systems of schools, nurseries, colleges, and universities across the world, created as they are by unequal societies, will forever to some degree reflect those societies. (Exley, 2016, p 128)

This point is echoed by Melissa Benn and Janet Downs:

> [T]o regard education as the main way in which disadvantaged pupils can rise economically is profoundly flawed. These changes will not happen unless other social and economic policies are in place. (Benn and Downs, 2016, p 15)

Finally, the findings of Kate Hoskins and Bernard Barker's qualitative study of students in two high-achieving schools add further weight to the argument:

> Upward mobility is either reserved for an exceptional few with pre-existing advantages (and so consists of the replacement of one elite with another), or dependent on economic expansion, driven by millions of students acquiring profitable new skills and earning new status within a much less steep social gradient. The first scenario does not seem to improve social justice, except for a select few, while there is strong historic evidence that the second may be desirable but is unattainable, especially at a time when inequality and disadvantage are increasing. (Hoskins and Barker, 2014, pp 148-9)

The shared note struck here – about the overriding importance of inequality itself, as a driver of class fate – is one to which we will return in both this chapter, and often in the rest of this book.

Meanwhile, what about the parents? What impacts does family background have on how kids get on? What do family autonomy and parental partiality have to do with class fate?

Is class fate parents' fault?

There are different ways of approaching this question. One is to look at how *forms* of family, or household structures, affect class fate – at how decisions or happenstance in family arrangements indirectly affect children's lives. Another is to look at how parental attitudes, privileges and decision making directly affect class fate – strategies of upbringing, for example, or the fabled use of parental 'sharp elbows' to advance the prospects of children. Another is to think about how family autonomy and parental partiality relate to other factors influencing social mobility (or lack of it). In this section, we will look at all three. It's worth noting as a starting point that family influence has already emerged here as a kind of flipside to the difference that educational institutions make, or don't make. We may expect to find a see-saw, so that where educational impact is lowest, in terms of patterns of intergenerational (im)mobility, family impact is highest. But things are more complex than that. And it's always possible that neither factor is crucial – and that the real action in ensuring that the kids of poor people are more likely to be poor lies elsewhere.

Family structure shifts historically. In the UK, for example, the proportion of families headed by a married or cohabiting couple fell from 92% in 1971 to 78% in 2011 (although the main dip happened between 1971 and 1998; the percentage has been fairly steady since). Meanwhile, the number of lone-parent families rose from 8% to 22% (having peaked at 25% in 1998). Twenty per cent of families with dependent children are now headed by lone mothers, of whom half have never married. The proportion of families with dependent children headed by a lone father has risen a little: it was 1% in 1971 and 2% in 2011 (ONS, 2011b). How these particular numbers and trends relate to social mobility can't yet fully be viewed in the rearview mirror. We may be able to see how recent variations in family structure work out for the children involved as children, but not as the adults they will later become.

Of course, since the 1970s, we have never been far from a periodic wave of media and think-tank angst over the risks posed by lone parenting and family instability to the well-being of children and the moral state of the nation (see, for example, Davies et al, 1993; Tinsley, 2014). As a series of riots in English cities was drawing to a close in August 2011, Prime Minister David Cameron already felt entirely confident in singling out the cause as a national state of 'moral collapse' in which 'children without fathers' were directly implicated (Stratton, 2011). Teenage pregnancies, single mothers and bad parenting line up alongside absent dads as regularly highlighted symptoms of social decline, moral disintegration and a crisis in the 'proper family' (Chambers, 2001, 2012). But we know that well-established stories can turn out to be shakier than common sense presumes. Beyond all the moral panics and choppy politics of family values, we might expect clear evidence of how shifts in family structure affect intergenerational inequality. Yet on the specific issue of the relationship between family form and life chances of children, the picture is mixed.

There is evidence that children from lone-parent families are more likely to experience poverty or be economically worse-off than their counterparts living in two-parent families (see, for example, Fischer, 2007). Household income is lower on average for lone-parent families with dependent children – around 91% receive income-related benefits, compared with 56% of their couple counterparts (ONS, 2010). Across member countries of the Organisation for Economic Co-operation and Development, average incomes for lone-parent families are less than half those of coupled families without children (Moullin, 2015, pp 193-4). But we also know that the risk of economic hardship differs from country to country, according to employment opportunities, levels of childcare provision, and the amount of financial support provided by the state and by estranged fathers (Chambers, 2012, pp 59-60). So it may be that income has more of an impact than number of parents. Surveying findings on the impacts of various aspects of family structure, Kitty Stewart concludes that 'while both low income and parental conflict make a difference to children's outcomes (and are associated with family structure), the *structure itself* does not appear to be very important' (Stewart, 2016, p 97; emphasis added). (An exception, she notes, might lie in reconstituted families: repartnering brings benefits in terms of household income, but not, it seems, in terms of outcomes for the children concerned.) We may know some decades hence what difference having same-sex parents makes to the life chances of children, but it's likely that there, too, income will emerge as a more decisive factor than family form.

But what about parenting attitudes and strategies – what parents *do* to and for their children – as opposed to parenting or household set-ups? We rather expect this to make a difference to children's life chances – and that with families left to their own devices, this will play out in different ways, with different outcomes for the children. We also expect those outcomes to boost some over others, in ostensibly unfair ways. As Harry Brighouse puts it,

[a]s long as children are raised in families, we know that their prospects will be profoundly affected by their family circumstances and conditions – that is by factors which do not flow from their level of talent or willingness to exert effort. (Brighouse, 2002, p 6)

And this happens well within the bounds of the acceptable range of treatment of kids. That's family autonomy for you. So among families where the children are neither neglected nor abused, and not in any way attracting the attention of child protection agencies, we will expect wide variations in the benefits children receive from the attitudes and strategies of their parents. Vallentyne and Lipson call this the assumption of family influence on the development of skills:

If consensual relations within a given family governing the development of its children are not coercively interfered with except to ensure for children the essential prerequisites for adult participation in society, then in general children with equivalent capacities will not have the same prospects for qualifications. (Vallentyne and Lipson, 1989, p 30)

Is this a reliable assumption? Parents themselves will certainly operate on this – perhaps assuming that everything done in the name of family autonomy is fair, and sometimes, more strongly, that in a competitive world, there's a kind of virtue in exploiting the uneven opportunities available to kids from different family backgrounds. Many cheerfully admit to being 'pushy parents', or 'tiger mums', to the extent that *not* being that way is implied to be a kind of mark of laxity (Carey, 2014). Those absentee fathers are culpable, in David Cameron's implied logic, partly because they're not using their 'sharp elbows', as he happily describes himself doing, to do the best by their kids (Hope, 2010).

These strategies start early; to return to our earlier example, the attainment gap between richer and poorer kids starts emerging even in their early years. While variations in children's outcomes and life chances may reflect individual variations in parenting styles, preferences and priorities, there are, over and above them, clear class patterns. The development of children's cognitive capacities is a key exemplar, already mentioned. Research has repeatedly shown that cognitive capacities develop more slowly in children from low social classes than in their counterparts in higher social classes. As one prominent British study has it, in a message we have already heard, by 120 months, the most able lower-class children at 22 months are overtaken by the weakest of children in the higher social classes at 22 months (Feinstein, 2003).

But gaps may set in even *before* the early years, prenatally. The developing foetus will already bear the imprint of its parents' socioeconomic position. Nutrition and protection at this stage are key to later health and development. Dietary deficiencies, exposure to chemicals, air pollution, living in poor housing – vulnerability to all of these will vary according to what parents earn. Poor housing, for example, is more likely to be unhealthy to live in, and more likely to be in areas where the general environment is less healthy for foetuses and babies. Of course, this is the very reason for statutory provision of prenatal support, and health visitor attention after birth – as exist in the UK. But the 'sharp-elbowed middle classes' are in a position both to make fuller use of such provision, and to supplement it as they see fit. The more we know about the ways in which children's brains develop, the more we know about how closely this is tied up with experience and exposure to environmental stimuli (Barry, 2005, pp 50-1).

And that exposure, those experiences, those stimuli are all, on balance, more available to foetuses, infants and children in better-off homes, with better-educated parents, and higher levels of cultural capital. From reading manuals on childcare to planning out days and weeks, reading bedtime stories and having longer, more detailed conversations – it all mounts up. Talk plays a crucial role: the amount of it, and its content. A much-cited US longitudinal study comparing talk in the homes of 42 families spread across four income brackets found that by the age of three, 86-98% of the words used by each child were derived from their parents' vocabularies. But the complexity of that vocabulary, and the deliberateness with which parents sought to expand that of their child, varied considerably according to class background. Most arrestingly, perhaps, the quantity varied too: 'in the everyday interactions at home, the average (rounded) number of words children heard per hour was 2,150 in the professional families, 1,250 in the working-class families and 620 in the welfare families' (Hart and Risley, 1995, pp 132-3). Whether resulting from conscious strategy on the part of the better-off, or just part and parcel of everyday interaction, the yawning vocabulary gap at age three between better-off and worse-off children paves the way for later class differentials in school performance.

Of course, the story doesn't stop at the age of three. Evidence of what happens next is provided by longitudinal ethnographic studies such as those compiled in Annette Lareau's *Unequal childhoods* (2011). Lareau's study of the experiences of children from 12 different families of varying class backgrounds in the same contemporary US city finds clear class divides in the ways in which children are brought up and oriented towards the world. 'For working-class and poor families,' she writes, 'the cultural logic of child-rearing at home is out of synch with the standards of institutions' (Lareau, 2011, p 3).

Middle-class children, parented via strategies described by Lareau as 'concerted cultivation', gain a sense of entitlement and confidence vis-à-vis the world beyond home and school, afforded by parental stress on reasoning, self-development and induction into adult modes of discourse and interaction. Meanwhile working-class and poor parents tend to pursue what Lareau calls 'the accomplishment of natural growth' – where the parent–child relationship features less dialogue, less micro-organisation of children's lives towards developmental activities, and more freedom for children to determine how their own leisure time is spent. Both versions of childhood may be happy; both afford opportunities to develop, albeit in different ways.

But by adulthood, there is only one set of winners in terms of entry into higher education and the job market. Middle-class children have been equipped in advance with the kind of 'cultural repertoire' that enables them to slip far more easily into the dynamics of the worlds of business and work. They have a confidence to contribute, and thus to achieve higher-status positions affording meaningful, fulfilling work and the realisation of potentials that, as we have seen, would have been evenly distributed among children of all class backgrounds at the outset.

Of course, these processes are not completely rigid or uniform. As Lareau says, 'Some working-class and poor youth, often with the assistance of an influential teacher, become first-generation college students. Armed with college degrees, they are able to defy the odds and become upwardly mobile' (Lareau, 2011, p 311). But these are variations: 'Middle-class families' cultural practices, including their approach to child-rearing, are closely aligned with the standards and expectations – the rules of the game – of key institutions in society' (Lareau, 2011, p 311). Lareau's work thus offers an answer to the ever-resonant opening questions of Paul Willis's 1970s study *Learning to labour*:

> The difficult thing to explain about how middle class kids get middle class jobs is why others let them. The difficult thing to explain about how working class kids get working class jobs is why they let themselves. (Willis, 1993, p 1)

Viewed on these lines, family autonomy (in its everyday workings, rather than as an abstract value) may seem more heavily implicated in the educational attainment of children from different backgrounds than school input is ever likely to be. Children with the same capacities will not have the same chances to develop qualifications. In a universal orphanage (Gheaus, 2009) or in Plato's nursery for the ruling class, such inequalities would not apply. And if positions are allocated on the basis of qualifications, children starting out with potentially equivalent capacities but brought up in families of different socioeconomic backgrounds will not have the same chances of realising that potential, or of achieving higher-status positions.

But it's worth pausing here, before confirming family autonomy as the chief vehicle of class fate. For what we're seeing here is an intimate entanglement between what happens in the name of family autonomy and legitimate parental partiality, on the one hand, and class, on the other. Family autonomy may certainly disrupt equal life chances all by itself, just because different parents do things differently in ways that affect the life chances of their children. But class and income inequality are massive accelerators and multipliers of those impacts, however painstaking the deliberations of parents about what is best for their children. Seeing family autonomy as the isolated architect of unequal life chances misses the fact this work can only take place, or take on pernicious dimensions, against a background of existing inequalities in class and income.

To put this another way, the reason that children in better-off families have better prospects is not only because their parents use family autonomy as a vehicle to promote those prospects, or indeed because of what goes on at school. It is also a symptom of the ways in which other goods are distributed – such as income and wealth – and opportunities are 'hoarded' for those of certain backgrounds (Wright, 2015, pp 6-8). If the intentions of individuals were the only factor at work, family influence itself would be sufficient to ensure that family autonomy serves to exacerbate inequality of life chances. But it is not sufficient by itself. Background conditions of structural economic inequality must also apply. Recent work by the Joseph Rowntree Foundation, surveying studies exploring the link between income and educational performance, has found strong evidence that 'children in lower-income families have worse cognitive, social-behavioural and health outcomes in part *because they are poorer*, not just because low income is correlated with other household and parental characteristics' (Cooper and Stewart, 2013, p 1; emphasis added).

What is at work here is something not traceable simply to the conscious choices of family members to promote the interests of their own; these must be indexed to the wider differential distribution of life chance-promoting goods and resources. The greater the levels of inequality in a society, the higher the stakes of family autonomy. Making children's starting points substantially more equal means paying 'careful attention to the overall level of inequality in society, and to the disparities in returns to different jobs, as well as working to reduce the extent to which childhood disadvantage holds back children's development' (Stewart, 2016, p 105). We are not in a climate where parents themselves are encouraged to pay that kind of attention – and it's not obvious that if they did, they could, through their choices, do much about those disparities. As John Hills concludes:

> It maybe should not be a surprise that there is a symbiotic relationship between high inequality in a society and low social mobility. In a highly unequal society, many advantaged parents will do all they can to ensure that their children do not slip down the economic ladder – they know that it goes a long way down. (Hills, 2015, p 215)

Or is it just the money, stupid?

We are building a picture here – the shape of an argument. It goes like this. There is a lot of class fate about: in the UK, relative social mobility has been fixed and low for decades (even when absolute social mobility was much healthier). Both educational practices and the everyday playing-out of family autonomy are accessories to this – perhaps especially the latter. But neither is sufficient. What is also needed, for a maximal constriction of the relative prospects of the worse-off (or 'maximally maintained inequality') is a background of persistent inequalities of class and income.

This is not, alas, orthodox 'social mobility' speak. Compare these two statements:

> This dense interconnection of family investment and access to good schooling lies behind our low social mobility. (Willetts, 2011, p 203)

> In Britain today, life chances are narrowed for too many by the home they're born into, the neighbourhood they grow up in or the jobs their parents do. (Clegg, 2011, p 3)

They are interestingly divergent, but both – in light of what we have discussed here – starkly incomplete. Neither couching of the problem mentions income inequality. Both feature in larger narratives where growing income inequality does not feature as part of the problem. So for Willetts, the class fate equation goes roughly like this:

Social immobility = uneven family influence + uneven access to education

This would suggest that promoting social mobility means evening up family influence, and evening up access to education. The latter has certainly been a stated aim since the 1945-51 Labour government. (One might also point out, however, that any project to minimise the impact of parents' socioeconomic position on their children's educational opportunity has been systematically undermined by the fetishisation, especially in England, of 'school choice' – which serves precisely to aid manoeuvring by parents into more advantageous market positions for their children.) But negating family influence is a far bigger ask. Attempts to do so have duly been far more sporadic. Perhaps the best recent example is the Sure Start programme, introduced and consolidated by the New Labour government of 1997-2010. By tooling up parents in more deprived areas to boost the learning potential of their pre-school children, this aimed – with some success – at compensating for the disparities revealed by the studies of class differences in vocabulary development and parenting styles mentioned above. But Sure Start, though vital, was bitty in terms of its geographical implementation. And it has since been cut back – by the very government of which Clegg was Deputy Prime Minister. It would take an exponentially pumped-up version of that kind of programme to make family influence less drastically uneven, in the way that Willetts' diagnosis of the problem requires.

Clegg's fuller picture of a recipe for narrow life chances – like the wider strategy in which that sentence features (HM Government, 2011) – also neglects to mention parental income, or inequalities of income in the social world into which those born in this or that set of circumstances will, in adulthood, emerge. Viewed this way, it is as if one's life chances are already set in place by virtue of one's immediate circumstances: one's family, one's neighbourhood, the jobs one's parents do. It is as if the spread of outcomes across society has no bearing at all. It makes it sound as if it's down to a legacy of poor preparation, poor choices, poor take-up of opportunities. It does not train its gaze on the availability of real opportunities, or the range of destinations they lead to, in terms of income, status and power.

Conclusion: mobility vs equality

The motif of a 'ladder' features often in social mobility talk. It carries great symbolic force. In Welsh, poignantly, the word for 'ladder' and 'school' is the same: *ysgol*. The image of a ladder ascending upwards carries the promise of limitless horizons: as many rungs as you are willing or able to climb, as many things as you are willing or able to learn. It is a neat-fitting emblem of aspiration. But it is viewable from other angles. Boliver and Byrne cite Raymond Williams' observation that a ladder is something that is climbed individually. Many from lower-class backgrounds 'indeed have scrambled up, and gone off to play on the other side' (Williams, 1963, cited in Boliver and Byrne, 2013, p 57). Others, in the process, have been left at the bottom – their position often entrenched by the very fact that their erstwhile rung-mates have climbed.

Williams happened to be writing in the swirl of the 'golden age' of social mobility. Discussing its subsequent halting – the story told in the earlier tables and figures, and their unpacking – Brian Barry notes that 'social mobility has become a zero-sum game: working-class children can rise only if an equal number of middle-class children fall, and this is barely occurring' (Barry, 2005, p 61). But ladders themselves come in different dimensions. If the rungs are very far apart – as currently, in Britain, with income inequality having been rising steadily since the late 1970s – the ladder takes on different dimensions. The gap between top and bottom rungs has grown beyond all expectation. Climbing the social ladder means taking increasingly large and unlikely leaps upwards. Talking about social mobility without talking about the scale of income inequality comes – as we shall see in the next chapter – uncomfortably close to blaming people for their own class fate. Blaming them, that is, for their not having leapt between rungs far further apart than has ever, historically, been the case.

Here, it is worth remembering that *any* social mobility measure needs handling with care. The measures themselves are rough and generalistic. There will always be cases that buck the trends, and beneath the broad sweep of any statistics, levels of nuance and ambiguity that make any individual life trajectory a far more complex thing than headlines about our socially immobile society will ever address. But, just as importantly, we must be wary of measuring the success of a life in terms of progress up through the class system. To speak of 'better destinations', 'bettering oneself' and indeed *'upward* mobility' risks installing a partial, one-dimensional sense of what it is to succeed, to feel fulfilled, or to lead a flourishing life. What counts as 'better' depends partly on what it is that you want to achieve. As is stressed by the ever-illuminating capabilities approach to social justice (see, for example, Sen, 1995, 2009; Brighouse and Robeyns, 2010), flourishing is achievable in plural ways. What facilitates it is not reducible to money, or educational success, or both. Both are necessary rather than sufficient conditions. The flipside of this is that – as with meritocracy, as we'll shortly see – talk of social mobility can have a flavour of in-built condescension. The immobile are somehow lacking or bereft. They have not had the chance to better themselves. Their children are ripe to be victims of the same sclerosis, socially stuck. Too much of this talk risks assuming (for example) that to live to one's full potential, only a university education, or an escape from one's humble beginnings, will do. These are issues to which we return in Chapters Four and Five.

So why has social mobility become such a reliable piece of shared vocabulary, across political parties? Why has the left, in particular, been so happy to invoke it? One enduring, reliable reading is that it allows a 'cop out from the challenge of creating a society in which outcomes are more equal' (Lipsey, 2015, p 23). Erik Olin Wright depicts the shift to social mobility talk like this:

> There was a great deal of concern about inequalities in the way people gained access to social positions, and certainly much

research on how hard life was for people living below the poverty line, but almost no concern with the magnitude of inequalities among the positions themselves. (Wright, 2015, p 128)

For Diane Reay, social mobility talk is not just a kind of negligence, but a piece of armoury:

> Britain in the 2010s is more unequal than Britain in the 1970s. And social mobility becomes even more important symbolically as inequalities worsen in societies. In deeply unequal societies such as the United Kingdom and the United States it operates as an effective form of symbolic violence, as a justification for growing levels of inequality. In the 2010s a majority of British people acquiesce in sharp distinctions of wealth and power on the basis that as individuals they are free to scale the heights. (Reay, 2016, p 29)

For Barry, the stalling of social mobility amounts to 'an undeclared but very real class war' (Barry, 2005, p 61). It's not just that it's undeclared; it is positively denied. One of the key ways in which this works is, as Wright and Reay suggest, by using the appeal of social mobility as a justification for inequality. This works best, as Wright suggests, when it is couched as a kind of equality itself – an equal chance to climb the ladder, whatever the scale of its rungs, or the ultimate gaps between those with more and less.

Note

[1] Comparable data on inequality is unavailable for Iceland, which is why it is not included in Wilkinson and Pickett's analysis.

FOUR

Unpacking equality of opportunity

Thus privilege, which was to have been exorcised by the gospel of 1789, returns in a new guise, the creature no longer of unequal legal rights thwarting the natural exercise of equal powers of hand and brain, but of unequal powers springing from the exercise of equal rights in a world where property and inherited wealth and the apparatus of class institutions have made opportunities unequal. (Tawney, 1920, p 37)

[I]n the absence of measures which prevent the exploitation of groups in a weak economic position by those in a strong ... the phrase equality of opportunity... is the impertinent courtesy of an invitation offered to unwelcome guests, in the certainty that circumstances will prevent them from accepting it. (Tawney, 1964, p 110)

Raymond Williams was quite right to question the ways in which the symbol of the 'ladder' gets woven into accounts of social progress. It's neither an accurate metaphor, nor as progressive as its users like to imply. Let's think instead about society not with a single scale of social positions, from bottom to top, but as something more multi-dimensional. We could think along the lines of economic, cultural and social capital. Along each of these lines, people will be ranked in different ways. Some people in their mid-30s – typically, exemplars of intergenerational upward mobility in very highly-paid work – may be top of the scale for economic and social capital, but closer to mid-table in cultural terms. They'll have more money and social connections than are fully exploitable in a single human life, but will rank lower than others in any hierarchy of the cultural elite. Others – say, graduates of a top university currently claiming jobseeker's allowance – will be socially networked and culturally omnivorous, but feeling the financial pinch.

Teasing out these three dimensions may suggest that to depict social class we now need three ladders, and three stick-figure versions of each of us, each perhaps differently placed on each ladder. But that doesn't seem right either. One reason for this is that, though distinct, the three aspects of class are intersectional. Each impinges on the other, in ways that may be different for each of us. As well as being desirable in itself, social capital can get you a 'good job'. Some 'good jobs', as well as bringing in high wages, are sources of induction into the cultural elite – of orientation into the ways of thinking and interaction that mark out the people who know the right things. (Of course, one wouldn't want to over-romanticise how easy it is to enter that world. As Suzanne Moore points out, key to the 'tiny, monstrous ways in which class functions' is that 'series of codes and signals that enable small gangs of people to recognise each other as clubbably employable, breedable' [Moore, 2016]. But an individual's cultural capital may rise even as they become painfully aware how far they remain from the upper echelons.) And one of the main uses of cultural capital is the potential leverage it gives, in opening up potential reciprocal relationships with others – greasing the wheels is partly how 'soft power' operates. So to be an accurate symbol, the three ladders would need to stand in some kind of twisty, overlapping relation, looking very little like ladders if at all.

Another reason is captured by Andrew Sayer, reviewing Savage's work. It's that as well as different dimensions of class standing in complex relations to one another, *individuals'* lives stand in complex relations to one another. Social reality is messier than clean class schemas will ever allow:

> [W]e need concepts of class that deal with *relations between* people: buyer and seller, employer and employee, lender and borrower, landlord and tenant, carer and cared-for. Most of these are unequal in terms of power, and many allow one side to take advantage of this, free riding on the efforts of the other.

Nevertheless, social reality is far too messy for us to expect them to crystallise out of neat classes of the sociological kind, not least because the amounts of money acquired with different class categories, and work done, can vary considerably – a small-time employer may earn less than a top employee of a big firm – but also because each of us is likely to enter into more than one of these relations. (Sayer, 2016, p 173; emphasis added. See also, on the outworkings of class, Sayer, 2005, 2009)

This relationality is difficult to do full justice to in diagrams or headlines, or even lengthy commentaries on class dynamics. As noted in the previous chapter, when we're talking about the different social positions that people end up in – vital, of course, to any measure of social mobility – we are always doing something simplistic. The same goes for talk about what it is to 'move up in the world'. There are different ways of thinking of 'up'. Making out that happiness or fulfilment lies mainly in having a higher-paid job may seem as partial or one-sided as saying that it lies mainly in having proper time to spend with one's grandchildren, or in knowing that one has a strong network of friends, or in watching the snooker on TV. What it is to be 'upwardly' mobile will always have a subjective component, just because each of us has different priorities. And it must always stand in connection to, rather than in isolation from, what it is to be 'downwardly' mobile, or stable.

All of this serves as a big disclaimer. Though the ladder is a problem, it's difficult to come up with a single alternative image to capture these different dimensions – except perhaps a very fiddly spreadsheet. Falling back on the Goldthorpe three-class schema will, for our purposes, do. The reason we need to do this is that we're now going to look at the notion of equality of opportunity – what it is that's supposed to be good about it, and what its limitations may be. To do that, we need to have an answer to this question: an equal opportunity for *what*? Let's say, for the sake of what follows, that we mean an equal opportunity to move up, or avoid moving down, between the three categories we set out in the previous chapter: salariat, intermediate class and working class.

Equality of opportunity's ready appeal

In a TV interview in 2013, George Osborne, UK Chancellor of the Exchequer, made a point the general flavour of which we encounter a lot. He said it in the context of a discussion both of the culture of excessive bonuses in the financial sector of the UK economy, and of recent comments made by Conservative MP and former London mayor Boris Johnson that equality is a futile aim and bad for the species, because too many human beings have an IQ of 80. His point went like this:

> There is increasing agreement across the political spectrum that you can't achieve equality of outcome, but that you should be able to achieve equality of opportunity. You should give everyone the best chance, and I think education is key to this. (Osborne, 2013)

In the immediate context of that comment, its significance is especially acute. People with an IQ of 80 should be given as equal a chance to get ahead (let's not say climb the ladder) as those with an IQ of 150. It's not that they should rightly travel as far. It's just that they should have the same starting line, with any rules governing the different life journeys of all those on that line applying consistently to all.

That's equality of opportunity, in a simple way. It's routinely contrasted with equality of outcome, or condition. A simple way to explain the difference is by way of a cake. You bring a cake to a room in which there are 19 other people, with a plan to distribute it fairly. Two plans occur to you. You can either divide it carefully into 20 pieces of equal sizes, and give one to each person, or give everyone a raffle ticket, blindfold yourself, draw a ticket out of a hat, and give the whole cake to the holder of that ticket.

The first option represents simple equality of outcome: everyone gets the same. The second option represents equality of opportunity: everyone has the same chance of success.

Osborne is entirely justified in pointing out the increasing degree of political preference for the second option. We've heard plenty of voices in this book already, reinforcing a clear convergence on this point – from New Labour (Gordon Brown and Alan Milburn), the Liberal Democrats (Nick Clegg) and now the long-serving Conservative Chancellor. The view will surface again. And it's backed up by plenty evidence from public opinion research – which is partly, of course, why 'equality of opportunity' is a value that politicians feel entirely comfortable to trumpet. When asked whether they agree or disagree with the statement that 'The fairest way of distributing wealth and income would be to give everyone equal shares', more people disagree than agree: 32% more in the UK, 51% in the US and (interestingly) 68% in Estonia. And when asked whether they agree or disagree with the statement 'It's fair if people have more money and wealth, but only if there are equal opportunities', far more people agree than disagree: 71% more in the UK, 88% more in the US and 96% in Estonia. In these three countries there are very similar results for the statement 'People are entitled to keep what they have earned – even if this means some people will be wealthier than others' (Marshall et al, 1999, p 246). The general public in Estonia, on this evidence, is possibly the most pro-equality of opportunity of any country one could imagine – and also, the most averse to equality of condition.

It's interesting to think of the moral psychology at work here. The figures themselves don't tell us why exactly *why* people are far readier to endorse the second statement over the first. And by themselves, they don't tell us whether people think that equality of opportunity actually exists, in their country. (As it happens, the same survey data showed that Americans mostly do believe that – and that they are about seven times as likely as British people to do so.) Perhaps most crucially, they don't tell us what people responding to the survey understand by 'equal opportunities' – or indeed, by 'more', when it comes to money and wealth. What reasons might people have for favouring the second option over the first? What other principles or values might be at work here? Here are some candidates:

- People should have an equal opportunity to do well. But not everyone *deserves* to do well.
- The amount of money and wealth different people have should reflect their talents and efforts.
- It's more efficient to have a society where the best jobs and highest rewards go to those best qualified to do them.

There is a strong 'fairness' component to these beliefs – one that is highlighted best if we think of a society in which the opposite principles apply. So, something like the following:

- People should not have an equal opportunity to do well. To ensure this, for example, the game should be rigged for some over others when we're allocating jobs. In fact, some positions should not even be accessible at all by people who come from certain backgrounds.
- Rather than reflecting their talents and efforts, the amount of money and wealth different people have should reflect circumstantial factors, and sheer luck – advantages that have fallen into their laps, rather than being earned in any obvious way.
- Efficiency is better served where the best jobs are done by under-qualified people.

Working with these values – both sets – tells us something about why social mobility seems so readily picked up by politicians. For there's strong sense of natural justice about what's at stake here. It is a kind of manifesto against 'opportunity hoarding' (to use Charles Tilly's term – see Tilly, 1998). If we're shocked that the elite professions are dominated by people from privileged backgrounds, for example, this seems very likely to be because there seems to be an intrinsic unfairness built into it. There is a bias in favour of those from certain backgrounds.

The game has been rigged, rather than it being a fair competition, in which all compete on equal terms. The playing field is not level.

Intergenerational inequality of opportunity

But at this point, one wishes that surveys like the one discussed in the previous section had added another dimension, when posing their questions – more specifically, that they included the intergenerational story, and factored in families and class fate. When we do that, the choice between the first and second statements no longer seems like a fork in the road. The two become entwined with each other. For as soon as one generation has run its course, unless we try to redistribute outcomes more evenly among their children, opportunities will not be equally generated in the next. Maybe the best way to illustrate this is by returning to a starting-line analogy.

Imagine we are in an alternative version of 22 July 2013, where there exists perfect equality of opportunity in the UK. The playing field is perfectly horizontal, and beautifully flat. Officially, the 2,000 babies born that day have an exactly equal chance to get ahead. So they start off at the same line. In our alternative version of society (it doesn't matter, for now, how far it is from the real version), there are guaranteed and clear rules, applied consistently to them all, making sure that as their lives unfold, none is subject to unfair discrimination. They are a representative sample, demographically: in terms of gender, race, religious beliefs, sexuality, disability and everything else, they are, at birth, an exact cross-section of society. And their parents came from all walks of life – the full range, in terms of levels of economic, social and cultural capital. Some of their parents were hermits. Some worked in call centres. Some lived like Margot and Jerry in 1970s TV sitcom The Good Life – self-consciously upwardly mobile. Some lived like Tom and Barbara in that same series – keen to 'downsize' to a simpler, less materialistic life. Some were landed gentry. Some were long-term unemployed.

But all of this, for our cohort on the starting line of life, is irrelevant to how the rules will treat them. They're a diverse bunch. So, of course, their lives will take shape according to their different aspirations, talents, motivations and efforts. But the rules will treat them entirely neutrally. Their socioeconomic backgrounds will not play a role in how their lives go. Their opportunities to get ahead are, when the starting whistle goes on their lives, entirely equal. We are witnessing what seems like some kind of perfect experiment in absolute social mobility. It won't be about where you came from. For this cohort of babies, it'll be entirely about what they're like as individuals, what their plans are, and where they're planning to go. They are all guaranteed a fair go. If we take the 10 dots in Figure 4.1 as standing in for the full 2,000, this is how they look, on the starting line of life.

Figure 4.1: The starting line in an 'equal opportunity' society: 22 July 2013

Now the whistle has gone. Our cohort set off from the starting line, and their lives unfold.

As we would expect, this happens in diverse ways. The date, 22 July 2013, happens to be the day on which Prince George was born, to parents William Windsor and Kate Middleton. So life for one of our cohort in particular will unfold radically differently from 'actual 2013'. George will inherit no advantages of status: the exceptional position of his parents will not shape his start in life at all. But apart from that, how his life goes will be tricky to predict. If 'alternative 2013' is statistically equivalent to our own, we have a good sense of the overall shape of the destinies of the cohort. One hundred and thirty, perhaps a little more, will go to private schools. Eight will die before their first birthday, of whom five will have lived in poverty. Twenty-five will be young carers. Two hundred and fifty or so will experience mental health problems before they are 18, among the 500 who do so during their lifetime (figures from Harle, 2013). But that's just the thing. Whether 'alternative 2013' would mirror 'actual 2013' at all is precisely the question, when thinking about what equality of opportunity means.

It could be that it means simply that society contains precisely the same pathways, but which are taken by whom is no longer determined by their background. There will be the same opportunities: it's just that who takes them up will not be predicted by their starting point in life, because everyone is starting on an equal footing. Perhaps, positions would come to people purely on merit (on which, more shortly). This world – where for one generation, the socioeconomic background of their parents has no direct bearing on their destination in life – is clearly drastically distant from our own. But in another version of 'alternative 2013', the gap is greater still.

For in that more complex version, the pathways too would be shaken up (as well as who takes which). They would not replicate, nor necessarily bear much resemblance to, those of 'actual 2013'. In fact, this makes more sense, if genuine equality of opportunity is to apply. For one thing, it's not clear whether there can be private schools in 'alternative 2013', unless places there are allocated by lottery – and even then, it's not clear whether their existence is compatible with everyone competing on a level playing field. (It depends, of course, on what you mean by a 'level' playing field, and how long it is supposed to stay in place.) Would anyone have died in infancy, in a society where everyone had an equal opportunity to succeed? Would mental health issues play out in the same way? It seems pretty unlikely. So many of the features of 'actual 2013' – so many contours and trends and statistics – reflect the fact that opportunities are not equal, that it's difficult to see how the contours of 'alternative 2013' would go. But if the likelihood of dying in infancy is currently closely related to one's social position at birth, and if in our alternative world such positions have been rendered equal, we can assume the numbers will change. If we had to bet on it, we'd assume they would be lower.

We may now be getting dazzled by counterfactuals – about what would be the case, if things were completely different. 'Actual 2013' is so saturated in the influence of family circumstances that the exercise of imagining that influence away is beginning to feel too much like science fiction, rather than something we can map out with any real assurance. But for sure, the picture we're getting is that 'alternative 2013' would be a very long way away from 'actual 2013'. The UK general public are right to be sceptical that equality of opportunity really exists in society as we live it. Something else is emerging. The idea that 'It's fair if people have more money and wealth, but only if there are equal opportunities' is beginning to look rather more complicated than it seemed. It doesn't, at face value, look *at all* compatible with the idea of a hereditary monarchy, unless the full version of the statement reads 'It's fair if people have more money and wealth, but only if there are equal opportunities for everyone apart from Prince George.' But among the public, support for the monarchy seems to sit on an entirely separate plane from belief about equality of opportunity. On 27 July in 'actual 2013', an opinion poll revealed that only 14% of the British public thought that the country would be better off without the monarchy (Hennessy, 2013). Between this, and the same public's strong support for equality of opportunity, it seems something has to give.

But let's allow our story to run on, as if we really can imagine a society where an individual's background really doesn't matter, in terms of how their life turns out. By the time they're adults in their 30s, any early variations in the lives of our cohort will have fanned out further still. They'll have gained different qualifications, taken different paths, set themselves different goals, at different kinds of level. Some will have achieved their ambitions. Some will have not. Some will have revised their ambitions along the road – adjusted their preferences, in light of life's experiences. Whatever they're doing, some will feel more fulfilled than others. In the course of all this, they will have earned different amounts. Let's, for the sake of the exercise, imagine them all at 37 – and distribute them according to wealth. The further to the right they are positioned in Figure 4.2, the greater the wealth they now have.

Figure 4.2: The cohort aged 37, in an 'equal opportunity' society: 22 July 2050

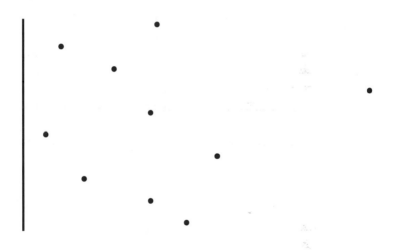

So they have travelled different distances, in terms of the accumulation of wealth. As the rules determine, this process has been entirely fair. None of them has been discriminated against on the basis of gender, race or disability. There is no determinate link between the destinations of these individuals and the incomes of their parents. Still, they sit in scattered places on the wealth chart. One, judging by how far ahead they are, seems to be a member of the '1%' – defined by Danny Dorling as someone earning upwards of £160,000 per year (Dorling, 2014, p 2). But even among the others clustered closer together, there are some fairly big gaps. Some will be home-owners; others not. Some will have substantial savings; others not. Some live in houses with spare bedrooms. One or two live in what estate agents eccentrically call studio flats – but in one case, because they live in an especially expensive city, the flat is basically the size of a large walk-in cupboard.

Now let's say that all of the people depicted become parents on their 37th birthday. On 22 July 2050, the successor generation is born, and their lives begin to unfold. The rules are the same: there'll be no unfair discrimination. Once again, how their life stories go will be entirely about what they're like as individuals, what their plans are, and where they're planning to go. But look at the new starting line. It's ragged. Some of those kids will start, materially, in entirely different worlds from others. There are advantages built in. The playing field is not level. To make it level, we would need to … well, we would need to have ensured that inequality of outcome for one generation does not mean inequality of opportunities for the next. We would need to have put equality of opportunity and equality of condition back together again.

Pondering this made-up situation, two things seem especially important. One is the sheer scale of the gap between 'alternative 2013' and 'actual 2013' – and indeed the actual version of any other year, anywhere. No human being has lived in a society with a genuinely level starting line (although some societies have come far closer to realising it than others). And the leap of imagination required to imagine people's lives unfolding without any kind of warping by unfair advantages stemming from family background is pretty demanding. We'd need perfect procedural rules to iron out discrimination, and they'd need to be enacted perfectly. In the mess of the real world, that's hard to picture. (It might also be hard to picture just in purely *ideal* terms, if that means coming up with a set of rules that everyone would agree were fair.) This suggests that 'pure' equality of opportunity is rather farther fetched than might be apparent, to many of its fans.

The other thing, more pressing here, is that as soon as we think in intergenerational terms, it seems we need to tie equality of opportunity and equality of outcome together. In other words, achieving anything like genuine equality of opportunity for the next generation would require a tight contraction of the range of outcomes of this generation. This issue runs like a thread through the backcloth of the whole discussion of social mobility in this book, and of how inequality runs in families. As Martin O'Neill puts it:

> It was common in the past for debates ... to be conducted between stylised positions that were labelled 'equality of outcome' and 'equality of opportunity'. But as the relationship between inequality and social mobility has come to be better understood, the uselessness of that distinction has become clear. Social mobility and (even approximate) equality of opportunity are possible only when the range of overall economic inequality is reduced. (O'Neill, 2016, p 95)

Getting here reinforces the conclusions of Chapter Three. It's looking very much as if 'social mobility' is not really the answer to social immobility. Class fate will not be undone just by giving people the chance to climb up through a stratified society. It will be undone, if it is, by changing the ways in which society is stratified. By lessening the gap between what people end up with. By paying attention, in other words, to the ways in which equality of condition, rather than being on some completely different plane, is always already implicated in equality of opportunity. But we do need to spend a bit longer on the latter, to figure out how all this sits.

Does 'equality of opportunity' actually mean two different things?

The previous section gave some space to what makes equality of opportunity a distinctive idea – but not so much to what *opportunity* actually means. Here's one simple definition:

> An opportunity to do something exists when there is there is nothing to prohibit it – so for example, a child has an opportunity

to be educated when there is no prohibition on their going to school; people have the opportunity for healthcare when there is no legal restriction on their accessing it; a person has an opportunity to get a job when they are not debarred from putting themselves forward for it.

Because the law tends to apply to people equally, it is easy enough to see how this converts into an understanding of *equal* opportunities. Going for a job gives the most familiar example:

> *Equality* of opportunity requires that jobs be allocated on the strength of people's *qualifications*, on their potential to do the job well, rather than other factors – like prejudice, nepotism, or disablism – entering into the decision. It exists when each candidate for a job is given fair consideration, on their own merits – and when the best candidate is appointed.

Here's an alternative definition of 'opportunity', adapted from Brian Barry (2005, pp 25-6, 37-8):

> An opportunity to do something exists for a person when there is some course of action lying within their power such that it will lead, if they choose to take it, to their doing or obtaining the thing in question.

There is a distinction here between a notional, abstract opportunity (in the first definition) and a really achievable one (in the second). On the first understanding, I have an opportunity to fly home by flapping my arms just as long as there's no legal prohibition or restriction on this. On the second understanding, that opportunity exists only if, by flapping my arms, I am actually going to find myself flying home. This makes a big difference in terms of how we understand equality of opportunity. In America, there has never been a prohibition on black people or women becoming president. Yet even without any such restriction, it took over 200 years for a black person to be in the position of realistically taking a shot at the presidency. As the time of writing (though this is about to change), no woman has run as a candidate. The notional, formal opportunity to run for president has existed for all American citizens since the country came into being. A *real* opportunity to do that, for women and black people (who of course make up the majority of US citizens) has been a longer time coming.

Viewed this way, the first version of opportunity comes to look rather more empty and abstract – and the significance of equalising it quite limited. Real equality of opportunity requires more than just that everyone in a pool of people has a notional chance to get a sought-after position in society. It means that everyone has a *real* chance to get that position. That's quite a different thing. It means having had a genuine opportunity to be the best candidate for that position. Some might push it further, like John Baker does, and say that a really egalitarian attitude towards opportunity would mean giving 'everyone the means to develop their capacities in a satisfying and fulfilling way' (Baker, 1987, p 49). This would mean that we knew that the pool of candidates for advantageous social positions really did represent the 'talent' out there in society.

As Barry fills in the point, the idea that appointing the best candidate embodies real equality of opportunity makes sense only if we can know that somehow lots of other people had a realistic chance of being the most qualified applicant. We'd then know that the person who was successful really was marked out by their superior choices from a set of options equally open to all of them. That's what would make the playing field level. So the best candidate would be the one who 'chose the right subjects to study, worked harder, and so on'. Without knowing that – or if we know, for example, if the best among the candidates happens to have been the one educated at a fee-paying school, with extra private tuition on top for the subjects in which they were struggling – we can't know we have equality of opportunity at all. Knowing that something like equality of opportunity has been obtained thus means looking further back in time, and beyond the pool of those who happen to have been in a position to apply:

[W]e should not confine our attention to those who had the minimum necessary qualifications at the time at which the job was advertised. Unless the claim of equal opportunity is to be a cruel hoax, we must also believe that there are millions of other people who could at some earlier stage have acquired the qualifications needed to get the job by making the right choices from a common set of options. (Barry, 2005, pp 39-40)

If we rewind to Figure 1.1, we will see Barry's point. We can see at 22 months that there will not be real equality of opportunity in a society like ours. If pre-school kids already bear the imprint of class inequality, it is simply wishful thinking – an empty, formal exercise – to talk of genuine equality of opportunity. Some talented kids, capable of becoming well-qualified applicants, will never had the real chance to get started down that road. They will have taken another – a story that those appointing to desirable positions can never be in a position to know.

So we need a rearview mirror to see whether opportunities have really been equal. Take a society where women have long been denied access to roles they could have fulfilled just as well as men if options had been genuinely open to them, from an appropriately young age. It's a society with a long legacy of routine sexism, and previously, of overtly sexist laws. Parents have tended to encourage girls not to seek a career, but to seek fulfilment instead in domestic duties and the care of a husband and children. But now, measures are taken to open up those forbidden roles to women. This will be done by ring fencing some roles for women – among what at first will be only a small pool of those who have, in the face of strong headwinds, become suitably qualified – to help redress the overwhelming gender imbalance in important sectors of the workforce. At the moment they hear the news, the would-be male candidate thwarted by the imposition of an all-woman shortlist may well feel unfairly discriminated against on the basis of his gender. But seen in the rearview mirror, the discrimination happened way back. It has been working in the other direction, against all those previous generations of women denied the chance to be that kind of worker. The all-woman shortlist is a way of *undoing* it – of finding a way of equalising opportunities, even if in a limited, imperfect way.

Two senses of meritocracy (and the trouble with both)

This points us towards a distinction between two different senses of meritocracy: a weaker and a stronger version. Here I'm going to condense a distinction made by Stuart White (2007, pp 56-64).

- *Weak meritocracy*: the absence of discrimination in access to important goods such as education and employment. Discrimination happens when a factor irrelevant to an individual's capacity to carry out a role is used as a reason to deny them access to it – in other words, when they are assessed on something other than their merits. So weak meritocracy is thwarted when, for example, a white candidate is offered a job rather than a better-qualified black candidate. Such discrimination could stem from the law: there could be overt prohibitions along lines of gender or religion, for example. But it is just as likely – and in the modern West (where we find increasingly robust anti-discrimination legislation such as the UK Equality Act 2010) more likely – to emerge in the practices of employers, or selective educational institutions.
- *Strong meritocracy*: the absence of discrimination in access to important goods such as education and employment, plus the elimination of barriers to becoming well qualified lying in people's upbringing. In a strong meritocracy, assessing individuals on their merits would mean eliminating disadvantages relating to inherited wealth, education and family environment. Children of the same potential would have the same chance to rise, regardless of how well-off their parents were. Schools would be arranged to avoid unfair advantage – a differential leg-up based on circumstance rather than merit – being bestowed through education. Any advantages stemming from parental cultural

capital, or parenting styles – the size of domestic vocabularies, whether parents are university-educated – would have been compensated for. Thus, people would really be assessed on their merits, rather than the degree to which they'd been blessed by happening to emerge from an environment conducive to success.

There are a couple of immediate things to note about this comparison. One is that weak meritocracy may no longer now look like *meritocracy* at all – not if meritocracy *really* means assessing people on their *merits* (rather than, for example, the lottery of birth), and people's merits being reflected in the positions they end up in. For it's perfectly compatible with weak meritocracy that the most prodigiously gifted people might never be discovered in the first place. We need no overt discrimination at all, for a boy from the wrong end of the class scale and the wrong end of the country not to end up as the top opera singer they could, given their native endowments, have been. We just need a lack of parental resources, maybe a domestic environment in which certain avenues aren't known about, or if they are, don't seem as if in a million years they're for 'the likes of us', an imperative to earn money early in life rather than pursue education, maybe cutbacks to local arts provision due to 'austerity' measures ... well, we know the story.

The other is that strong meritocracy is a rather massive, revolutionary-looking, deal. If it's persuasive as a doctrine, a society based on merit, where anyone can get where they want to go, where a person's background has no bearing on her ultimate destination, seems very far off. America, of course, once thought of itself as that kind of place. Indeed, Robert Putnam suggests that maybe in the post-war era, at least in his hometown of Port Clinton, Ohio, it came somewhere near to an approximation of it. Now, it is anything but. The life chances of Port Clinton kids has become drastically stratified. The basic reason is that the gap between richer and poorer families has grown exponentially in the 55 years since 1960. Those families channel privilege in ever grander and more overt ways, so that at high schools, all the most expensive cars now belong to the best-off students rather than their teachers. And yet the self-image of America, even among those American kids whose chances of being judged on their merits are in a steady state of recession, is of a meritocracy (Putnam, 2015). This is less and less because of discrimination in the law, or by the state, or by formal decision-making channels, or something that can be calibrated at the level of decisions, choices, or individual lives. It is more and more because of the sheer, chasmic structural inequality that, as in the UK, has accelerated since the 1970s into something way off the scale of what would previously have been imagined, let alone seemed acceptable. In the face of this, an appeal to weak meritocracy seems like the wrong answer to a different kind of problem.

But if it's bad form to say that America isn't meritocratic even when it clearly isn't, it's even worse form just to whisper, even with one's hand over one's mouth, what strong meritocracy would seem to require. As we've seen already but hardly needed to mention, the abolition of the family doesn't sit well with common sense. But if strong meritocracy is real meritocracy, stopping inequality running in families seems to be just *exactly*, as a basic starting-point, what meritocracy requires.

We should pause here a minute. This doesn't mean that strong meritocracy equals social justice. For one thing, it might be that there are social justice reasons to hang onto the family. We might think that people occupying social positions on genuine merit is a key part of what social justice means, but insist that social justice also means *other* things too – and that one of those is to do with family autonomy. Or we might (as we saw earlier) think that justice is only one side of the story anyway – that there is a whole other language of care that sits separately to it, but is of equal importance.

And on the other hand, we might question whether meritocracy – even in its most muscular form – is, in social justice terms, all that. Maybe we don't want to enshrine merit as the guiding principle of a just society. Why not? Well, here's a basic reason, articulated by Owen Jones:

> The idea of meritocracy ends up being used to justify or rationalise inequality. You say basically, inequality is deserved. The people at the top are there because they worked

hard, they're more intelligent, they're brighter, they pulled themselves up by their bootstraps. And those at the bottom are there deservedly too, because they're not as bright, they failed to get on, they don't have the same effort or determination or grit.... It's because if you do have such a grotesquely unequal society, you do have to find ways of justifying it. (Jones, 2013, at c. 37 minutes)

There are two sides to the dubiousness of the assumptions Jones describes. In the first place, it's not at all clear that there's any justification, in social justice terms, for the 'top' being a very long way from the 'bottom'. In 2016, the typical chief executive of a FTSE 100 company earns 180 more than the average full-time worker (Shaddock, 2016). Is it possible that they are worth it? Let's cash out what that would mean, via some notional finely tuned 'meritometer' fit to quantify the calibre and performance of different individuals. It would mean that those CEOs are 180 times as talented (or intelligent, to use Jones's own word), and put in 180 times as much effort, as the average full-time worker. Maybe they did 180 times as well in their maths GCSE, or have 180 times as much charisma, or are 180 times as good at making a decision, or closing a deal.

Or maybe, on the other hand, the rank unlikeliness of every statement in the previous two sentences suggests that it is *flatly impossible* to imagine any one worker being 180 times as good at anything as any other worker. Perhaps there is another language in which we might justify that kind of wage gap. But the language of merit does not seem to do it. Put like this, these are objections against promoting the belief that we live in a society where people's social positions reflect their merits, when really we don't live in that kind of society (because, for example, no one human being can conceivably 'merit' 180 times as much as any other). Sustaining them might suggest that the goal of meritocracy itself is entirely acceptable – it's just misapplying the term to our own society that is the problem. Maybe, if the world were already fairer, meritocracy talk would fit it. But in any society that has not already achieved social justice, talk of meritocracy is not a solution, but a kind of smokescreen, serving to reinforce any tendency to presume that the worse-off have been proven to be inferior.

So on the other side of the dubiousness of meritocracy lie the *effects* of those assumptions, on those at the bottom, and on society as a whole. There's an inherent risk that if we believe in it hard enough, if it becomes installed as the official description of the status quo, meritocracy 'ends up becoming a rubber-stamp for existing inequalities, re-branding them as deserved' (Jones, 2011, p 97). Talking as if we live in a world where people really do deserve their social positions is particularly pernicious when we so patently *don't* live in that world — and by itself offers no kind of route to meritocracy. In fact, it may amount to a roadblock. So as James Bloodworth puts it, 'the more meritocratic Britain becomes (or, to be more precise, the more Britain believes it is a meritocracy), the less sympathy there will likely be for those who find themselves at the bottom' (Bloodworth, 2016, pp 134-5). The ideology of meritocracy legitimises unconcern for society's 'losers'. Indeed it valorises it.

The points of Bloodworth and Jones echo the sentiments of the term's coiner — Michael Young, author of the Labour Party's 1945 election manifesto. A satirical ingredient key to his own depiction of meritocracy has been rubbed off by continuous usage, especially in its appropriation by its fans. Young's 1958 book *The rise of the meritocracy* is presented as a spoof, and as a dystopia — written retrospectively from a version of the 2030s where the principle of allocating places in the social hierarchy on merit really has been in operation for decades. This society is hierarchical, but in a way based on merit. It is a society where class fate can no longer be blamed on bad luck, or society. It is now absolutely, purely, the individual's doing. Previously, '[e]ducational injustice enabled people to preserve their illusions, inequality of opportunity fostered the myth of human equality' (Young, 1958, p 85). In a society based on merit, true human inequality is laid bare. The social ladder remains, but where this or that individual sits on it is entirely a matter of merit: 'Intelligence and effort together make up merit (I+E=M)' (Young, 1958, p 94). We know exactly who is inferior: '[t]oday all persons, however humble, know they have had every chance' (Young, 1958, p 86). So it's not just that if we believe we already live in a meritocracy, dismissal of the credentials of those with least will seem fair enough. It's also that if we really did live under pure meritocratic conditions, such judgements would become a kind of orthodoxy, perhaps even barely worth stating. Those on the lower rungs really would be worth less.

Meanwhile, back in our less than meritocratic world – a world in which, to Young's regret, much of what he predicted 'has already come about' – the belief that we live in one carries on its pernicious work. It thrives, not least, because it rather suits those at the 'top', earning 180 times the average, to believe that they are 'worth it':

> If meritocrats believe, as more and more of them are encouraged to, that their advancement comes from their own merits, they can feel they deserve whatever they can get. They can be insufferably smug, much more so than the people who knew they had achieved advancement not on their own merit but because they were, as somebody's son or daughter, the beneficiaries of nepotism. The newcomers can actually believe they have morality on their side. (Young, 2001)

The evidence of the previous chapter would, one would hope, make clear how wrongheaded that belief remains. We see in the transition from Young's original satire to the contemporary hailing of meritocracy a flipping and contortion of the term's purpose. Jo Littler describes the shift like this:

> It has moved from a disparaging reference to an embryonic system of state organisation creating problematic hierarchies through a dubious notion of 'merit', to a celebratory term connecting competitive individualism and an essentialised notion of 'talent' with a belief in the desirability and possibility of social mobility in a highly unequal society. (Littler, 2013, p 68)

One response to all this, in defence of meritocracy, might go something like this. 'OK,' the meritocrat might say, 'so the ideology of meritocracy is self-serving for the winners, and lousy for the losers. It inflates the self-worth of the former, and it shrinks the horizons of the latter. And it leads to smugness and snobbery. And it can serve to legitimate quite drastic inequality. But actually, those are prices worth paying. Because a society in which the best people have the best jobs – have most responsibility, make the big decisions, are generally steering the ship – is a society where everyone, in that respect, wins. And let's face it, that's a pretty important respect. Who wants those with *least* merits to be steering the ship? Nobody does. Not even those with least merits want that, if they know what's good for them.'

There does seem to be some weight to this. Who wants a society where the *less* competent surgeons or airline pilots or civil engineers are in charge? Maybe a bit (or indeed quite a lot) of unfairness is worth it, just because of the sheer social utility (the benefits to everyone) of having the best people – the experts – handling the most crucial and difficult jobs?

Up to a point, yes. Yet as Anca Gheaus has pointed out, this may largely depend on the job. For one thing, not all jobs require the very most talented to occupy them, in order for them to be done optimally. So yes, we want the most talented at medicine to be doctors. But we don't need the most talented solicitors to be solicitors. Past a certain point of competence, being utterly exceptional at being a solicitor adds no social utility whatsoever. We just need solicitors who are *good enough*. But there is a second, bigger point here. It applies to any unjust society – any messy and compromised society that has not somehow perfectly realised the principles of social justice, which is to say, any society going. People living in such societies 'have reasons *not* to want the most talented people to occupy those desired positions that are connected to the exercise of power' (Gheaus, 2014; emphasis added). Why? Because in the case of some jobs, in those circumstances, the better people are at them, the more social damage they do. So, for example, 'the most talented lawyers serving a corrupt legal system are likely to do more damage than more mediocre ones; the most talented conservative politicians will be most efficient at keeping in place unfair institutions; and similar things can be said about the most talented bankers, tax advisers and top managers working in unjust societies' (Gheaus, 2014). It might be good for *them* to occupy those positions, and for those whose interests this directly serves. But it is not good for society in general. Talent rising to the top is by no means unquestionably a good thing.

'So,' concludes Gheaus (2014), 'it seems a mistake to worry too much about social mobility. We should be a lot more worried about substantive inequalities than about the distribution of chances to end up as a winner rather than as a loser.' Here, as they say, we are again.

Conclusion: equality vs mobility, again

This chapter has mostly been conducted at quite a conceptual level. From different angles, we have been working away at the point that in fact, equality of opportunity is in a state of mutual entanglement with something usually taken to be its ideological rival: equality of outcome, or condition. The idealised model in which they are severed would be a pure meritocracy – with its sole stress on equality of opportunity. As White sums it up: 'For the meritocrat, maintaining equality of outcome would be unjust because it would entail a failure to give some workers the higher incomes than they supposedly deserve' (White, 2007, p 56).

We know this view is common. The clean separation of equality of opportunity from equality of condition is a reverberating trope. It loomed up, for example, in a recent contribution to 'Thought for the Day' on Radio 4's Today programme. In it, Rabbi Jonathan Sacks was teasing out the distinction, central to the Hebrew Bible, between two senses of justice: *mishpat*, meaning individual justice, and *tzedek*, meaning social justice. This distinction is indeed, as he suggested, a vital contribution to the world. Here's how he unpacked the idea of *tzedek*:

What it means is that we are all equal in the sight of God. We all bear his image. We are all created in his likeness. And society should in some way reflect this, not necessarily in terms of wealth or power, but at least in dignity and opportunity. It was perhaps the first attempt in history to break away from the social hierarchies that appeared with the birth of cities and civilizations, and it's been an inspiration to the West for many centuries. (Sacks, 2016)

I mention this not to create a diversion into the interpretation of religious scripture, but to note the freight carried by the note of equivocation in that fourth sentence. 'Not necessarily in terms of wealth or power, but at least in dignity and opportunity.' What happens when we unpack the notion of equality of opportunity is that the need for equivocation falls away. Access to dignity is *conjoined* with the distribution of wealth and power. Wealth and power are increasingly – and to an extent unimaginable at the time the writing of the Bible – a part of the *currency* of opportunity.

This is particularly definitive of our own, yawningly unequal times, where there is a new and massive scale to the uneven distribution of dignity, and where the idea that we are all created equal, whatever our circumstances or family background, seems particularly idealised. In modern capitalist societies, as David Marquand writes, 'poverty, homelessness, exploitation and degrading working conditions are the chief sources of humiliation' (Marquand, 2013, p 212). They are such, in part, *because* of the prevailing language of opportunity – and the assumption that people are where they deserve to be. The existence of the poor is, of course, an affront to the idea that somehow free choice in free markets benefits everyone:

The poor ought not to exist. Since they do exist, and since the ideology of untamed capitalism is assumed to be true by definition, the only possible explanation is that they have failed to take advantage of the opportunities that free markets have given them: that they are to blame for their own poverty. In days gone by a supposed distinction between the 'deserving' and 'undeserving' poor was a stock theme of public debate. Now there are no deserving poor: there are only the undeserving poor and 'hard-working families who play by the rules'. (Marquand, 2013, p 141)

If we're not careful, the rhetoric of equality of opportunity, severed from equality of condition, will serve to strengthen that wedge between hard-working families and the undeserving, and to help write the latter off. Such are the dangers of speaking of equality of opportunity as a kind of given, already achieved, in a context where, as Tawney puts it, 'property and inherited wealth and the apparatus of class institutions have made opportunities unequal'. This is not just a moral point. When we consider the extent to which being worse off runs in families, and the extent to which it is delivered by the luck of the circumstances of upbringing, concluding that the poor, in some general sense, *merit* being that way, and at such a distance from the top, seems, simply, factually illiterate.

And yet a severing of the two kinds of equality runs like a thread through social mobility talk, where the idea that it's only *unmerited* inequalities of income that are problematic. So as Nick Clegg (again) has it:

Social mobility is what characterises a fair society, rather than a particular level of income equality. Inequalities become injustices when they are fixed; passed on, generation to generation. (Clegg, 2010)

Throughout this book, we have been stacking up reasons why this claim is a mistake. This point by John Goldthorpe echoes what we found in the previous chapter:

In sum, attempts at increasing equality of opportunity, in the sense of a greater equality of mobility chances, would seem unlikely to be effective, whether made through educational policy or otherwise, unless the class-linked inequalities of condition on which class mobility regimes are founded are themselves significantly reduced. (Goldthorpe, 2012, p 19)

By now, we've seen a great many different factors that back that claim up. Inequality runs in families not simply because of what *families* do, but also, and chiefly, because of what *inequality* does, and how it works. What, if anything, might we do about either?

FIVE

Towards real equality of life chances?

Our story so far goes like this. Almost everyone seems to have a problem with a society in which family background plays too big a role in people's life chances. And plenty, prominent voices in policy included, are happy to say in response that we should try to equalise life chances. The family poses a major hurdle to any such project, as well as pressing on us a complex package of other issues pertaining to social justice, because it tends to push back against the achievement of equality. The family is a major engine of class fate. Class fate is rife, and particularly so in countries like the UK that are characterised by widening income inequality. Some people think that all we need for social mobility is genuine equality of opportunity. Yet the latter, though prominent in political rhetoric, is far scarcer and more intermittent in the lived reality of societies such as the contemporary UK. And the meritocracy to which it is often allied is neither as tenable nor as appealing as its widespread endorsement might suggest. Equality of opportunity seems in important respects to be unachievable without greater equality of condition. Social mobility, as an aim, does not, in the end, seem a good yardstick of any kind of equality.

So we've built up a picture where social mobility is not itself the answer to class fate. Where does that leave the family, then? And if the redistribution of wealth looks like (at least) a substantial part of the answer, why doesn't social immobility get tackled that way?

Talking life chances without talking redistribution, or the family

James L. Fishkin defines equality of life chances like this:

> According to this notion, I should not be able to enter a hospital ward of healthy newborn babies and, on the basis of class, race, sex or other arbitrary native characteristics, predict the eventual positions in society of those children. (Fishkin, 1983, p 4)

In the US of 1983, as he points out, those predictions could all too confidently be made. From what we've seen in this book, the same is true of the UK in the early 21st century. Fishkin presents this definition as one horn of a 'trilemma' facing liberal egalitarian theorists of social justice – a kind of dilemma with three corners. There are three principles crucial to liberals that cannot be fully realised in conjunction. Or, more precisely, commitment to any two of them rules out commitment to the third. Equality of life chances is one. We have spent a fair bit of time with the other two already, in different guises. Fishkin phrases them like this:

> *The principle of merit*: positions should be awarded via impartial evaluation of qualifications. There should be 'fair competition among individuals for unequal positions in society'. (Fishkin, 1983, p 19)

> *Autonomy of the family:* 'consensual relations within a given family concerning the development of its children should not be coercively interfered with except to ensure for the children the essential prerequisites for adult participation in the society' (Fishkin, 1983, pp 35-6)

So Fishkin's case is that between these three, something has to give. One of them must stand aside, in order for the other two to be realised. It's worth noting here that he has effectively split equality of opportunity into two separate components: the principle of merit, and equality of life chances. Fishkin's point is that if you really want to secure the latter, while respecting family autonomy, you need to let go of the idea that everyone going for positions will be judged impartially, on the basis purely of their qualifications. You need to be willing to give extra leverage to those from disadvantaged family backgrounds.

Our job is not simply to confirm or deny the horns of the trilemma – partly because that's not a simple business at all, and would require a long excursion into political philosophy. But I do want to place it on the table, for a particular purpose. It flags up a problem that, in political discourse, tends overwhelmingly to be swerved around or wished away. Here's Nick Clegg again, with two points we have already cited separately, but are now worth putting together:

> In Britain today, life chances are narrowed for too many by the circumstances of their birth: the home they're born into, the neighbourhood they grow up in or the jobs their parents do. (Clegg, 2011, p 3)

> Social mobility is what characterises a fair society, rather than a particular level of income equality. Inequalities become injustices when they are fixed; passed on, generation to generation. (Clegg, 2010)

For Clegg, the first offers a kind of tableau of unfair advantage, confirmed by the final sentence of the second. The key to a fair solution is the first sentence of point two. Isolating these points isn't to pick on Clegg, or make a special example of him. His stance is entirely typical among various purveyors of social mobility talk encountered in this book. These quotes make a neat summary of a position to which, especially since 1997, the UK's political mainstream has cheerfully signed up.

Why is it so very attractive, as a stance to take? One basic reason is that Clegg is a politician. Why do politicians prefer to talk about equalising life chances rather than, for example, reducing income inequality? And why, when they're doing that, do they tend to insist that education is the key to achieving those more equal life chances, rather than (again) reducing income inequality, or trying to combat the ways in which privileged families tend to preserve their privileges, even when educational opportunities are opened up for all? Why don't they speak freely about the lack of 'room at the top' meaning that there's now a door policy of 'one in, one out' when it comes to entry into the salariat – so that we need to engineer some downward mobility in order to allow for some upward mobility? For quite a basic reason. We're arriving back at the three items of 'common sense' with which we started: that the family is natural and sacred, that social mobility is by definition a good thing, but that of course, every child deserves a fair go. Referring to life chances allows politicians to embrace the second and third of these, without threatening the sacred status of the family, and without talking about redistribution.

Talking redistribution would seem the obvious response to all that we have seen of the impacts of socioeconomic factors on class fate. Arguably, we can take the sting out of the tension between family autonomy and equal life chances by reducing the gap between rich and poor – by lowering the stakes of what family influence can do, by making the gap between different children's eventual conditions smaller (see, for example, Calder, 2016). Promoting family autonomy would look rather more like a victimless celebration of the sheer plurality of possible versions of human living, were it not set against a backdrop of drastic class inequality. And we can assume that reallocating economic capital will have at least some loosening effects on the intermediate and salariat classes' grip on relevant types of social and cultural capital too. But substantial redistribution of this kind is, at least under current horizons, politically unlikely.

One reason why redistribution is not the favoured policy lever, in the face of greater social immobility, is that among the voting public, downward mobility is a threat now in a way that it never was in the post-war 'golden age'. Peter Mandler expands this point from a historian's perspective:

> The problem is that it is more difficult to sell politically a redistributive policy than it was in the 1950s, for the same reason that downward mobility is more of a threat today – there are too many people in the middle…. Today, in Britain,

after three generations of upward mobility, most people have experienced it already and are understandably reluctant to abandon it.... Redistribution that focused on those top few percentiles wouldn't go very far in fostering social mobility. (It might have other advantages.) Redistribution that went much further again asks too many people to give up privileges that they may rightly feel have been hard won by themselves and their parents. The golden age of social mobility was almost certainly a one-off. We can't go there again. (Mandler, 2016)

Fear of dropping down among people in the middle is, on this hypothesis, the biggest barrier to tackling class fate by seeking to reduce income inequality. Though income inequality has increased exponentially, only a relative few are super-rich. There are good reasons why those in the middle may be keenest to sharpen their elbows.

Unsharpening elbows: factoring the family back in

Meanwhile, tackling social immobility by confronting family influence on life chances is barely any easier a policy nettle to grasp. Politicians and policymakers tend mostly to deal with Fishkin's trilemma by ignoring it. It comes far more easily to extol the virtues of merit and equal life chances than to start tampering with family autonomy. As a result, the trilemma haunts social mobility talk, which takes place as if all we're trying to do is combine merit with equality of life chances, without having to confront the fact that family autonomy, if we want it too, seems to confound the very chance of having both. Politicians seem unlikely to start flag waving for reducing family choices any time soon.

But what if we *did* bite that bullet, and confront family autonomy? There are compelling grounds on which to do so. We have seen that what goes on within families, and the decisions parents make on behalf of their children, are incubators of unfair advantage and disadvantage among children and the adults they become. There is every reason to endorse Okin's verdict that the sheer extent to which elements of family background determine the shape of our lives means that '[a]ny claims that equal opportunity exists are … completely unfounded' (Okin 1989, p 16). In the introduction, we noted that parents' right to pursue, sharp-elbowed, their child's advantage carries a good deal of weight as a 'common-sense' entitlement. But then at the end of Chapter Two, we considered various possible places to draw the line around legitimate parental partiality – to delimit what parents may do to advantage their kids at the expense of others. Those issues are worth returning to. With regards to politicians grappling with those questions, well, we wouldn't want to hold our breath. But analysts of ethics and social policy can certainly wade in. In their comprehensive work *Family values: the ethics of parent-child relationships*, Brighouse and Swift (2014) do just that. Their approach is illuminating, in our context. Some relevant aspects are worthy of a brief synopsis (see also Calder, 2015).

Their approach rests on an appeal to *relationship goods* – specifically, 'the goods distinctively made possible by familial relationships' (Brighouse and Swift, 2014, p x). Parent–child relationships are unique, or anyway distinct in their value: the family 'produces certain goods that would otherwise not be available, or in some cases, would be much more difficult to produce' (p 57). But children's interests in growing up well take ethical precedence over parents' interests in achieving the distinctive goods of parenting. This is because of what it is like to be a child. Children are profoundly dependent on others for their well-being, vulnerable to others' decisions, and, when young, 'lack a well-developed and stable distinctive conception of what is valuable in their life' – though are also in the process of developing 'capabilities that enable them to realize their own interests' (p 62). They have an interest in developing that way, and being protected and nurtured to that end.

Against this background, do parents have a right to confer advantage on their children? To use their sharp elbows? No they don't – not as such. They only have rights to do things that are actually essential for the realisation of familial relationship goods. What does that mean? It means a 'yes', for instance, to the reading of bedtime stories, because this embodies a certain uniquely valuable feature of the parent–child relationship. This kind of exclusive attention, at a particularly important time of day, in a way which reinforces mutual identification, is part of the distinctive value of parent–child intimacy. It is emblematic of why children have an interest in creating a stable, ongoing relationship with a parental figure, and is a likely building-block of the forging of that relationship. But doesn't the reading of bedtime stories confer advantage on children – for example, compared with those children who don't get bedtime stories? Yes it does. But in this case, that advantage is legitimate. It is part and parcel of the realisation of a relationship good. So what *don't* parents have the right to do, by way of conferring advantage for their kids? Anything that isn't essential to the realisation of such a good.

> Think of a parent who invests all possible resources in securing competitive advantage for his child: perhaps, say, sending her to an expensive private school designed to optimize her chances in the competition for well-rewarded and interesting jobs, investing in a trust fund, and interacting with her on the basis of judgements about how best to develop her human capital. These activities are not protected by the considerations we have invoked concerning the value of the family. In normal circumstances at least, none of these is essential for the parent to carry out her special duty of care for the child – none is essential for the child's fundamental interests to be adequately met – and none is essential for the important goods distinctively made available by the familial relationship. (Brighouse and Swift, 2014, p 125)

Bequeathing property sits in the same category as sending one's kids to private school. The point here is not about the scale of the advantage that accrues to the child over others of their generation. Bedtime stories disrupt equality of life chances just as much as fee-paying education does. But the first is protected as a parent–child interaction, not because it confers competitive advantage. Parents 'have rights to interact with their children in particular ways, but they do not have rights to bring about the distributive outcomes that result from the way those attributes currently interact with, for example, the labor market or the tax and transfer system' (Brighouse and Swift, 2014, p 130).

This 'take' on the limits of parents' right to advantage their kids is not, naturally, the only one in town. But it's highly illuminating both in navigating Fishkin's trilemma, and in thinking through the mechanics of class fate. We've seen that the more unequal a society, the greater parents' motivation to bolster their child's prospects, to avoid a drop down the ladder, or to maximise their chances of moving up. Generally, the stakes of not doing so rise in proportion to the scale of the gap between those with more and less. Kitty Stewart concludes:

> How can policy prevent income and wealth from being used by better-off parents to cement their children's position? Only by what James Fishkin has argued to be a 'sacrifice of family autonomy'. This might involve, for example, the abolition of private education and private tuition, lotteries for school places, an end to inheritance and to financial gifts to the next generation. These policies might help [in] … preventing the distribution of income from dominating the distribution of goods in other spheres, including the health, educational success, and job opportunities of children. (Stewart, 2016, p 105)

Thus a similar conclusion is reached from different directions by social policy analysts such as Stewart, by theorists of distributive justice such as Fishkin, by theorists of the ethics of the family such as Brighouse and Swift, and by analysts of social mobility such as Goldthorpe. The converging conclusion is roughly this: that when the tensions between equality and family autonomy bite hardest, it's on the side of the latter that something has to give. Not everything, by any means: Brighouse and Swift preserve a clear sphere of legitimate privilege, in those practices – as in the altogether non-trivial example of bedtime stories – essential to the realisation of familial relationship goods. But still, thinking through the ethical limits of family autonomy means jettisoning a good deal of what in the 'common-sense' lexicon of family entitlement might seem sacred.

Factoring the family back into our discussion of life chances, you can see why politicians prefer to leave it out. Turning from the finer points of academic analysis to the different scale and rhythms of the public realm, we find reflected back at us a thin, one-sided, point-avoiding public discourse on the contours of a fair society, and the place of family privilege within it. There is little to question the presumption that as long as family relations do not involve neglect or abuse, what goes on under the auspices of family autonomy is always legitimate. What proportion of voters would support what needs to be done to realise the equality of life chances they genuinely agree to be a part of social justice 'common sense'? If it's not many, opinion formers are as culpable as those most eager to agree with them.

Conclusion: three modest suggestions

So there we are: talking about equalising life chances without talking about either substantial redistribution of wealth, or limiting family choices, has condemned a generation of politicians to being resoundingly ineffectual in tackling social immobility – at the same time as they happily proclaim this to be the very holy grail of politics. What is to be done, in the direction of real-life equality of life chances? In such a climate, it's as well not to start with the biggest, most effective, most *prima facie* desirable proposals – the kinds of thing that, as Stewart says, would really neutralise the sting of family privileges, and achieve the kind of fairness that altogether minimises the influence of family background on how people's lives turn out. So I won't be reaching straight for the abolition of private schools, or lotteries for school places, or large bequests to family members – notwithstanding the imposing force of the ethical case for doing just those things. The making of that case is a larger-scale job for a sequel discussion.

Instead, here are three more modest, brief suggestions for areas of attention – none of them original, but each of them some way from being realised (or indeed, in the first and last cases, initiated). These are policies that could feature in an easily imaginable manifesto for a political party with hopes of electoral success; policies that – so we might hope – might find favour if subjected to an even moderately open and rational process of public deliberation. Having said which the first, at least, would make the *Daily Mail* scream.

1. Replacing inheritance tax with an accessions tax

If there's one thing that's neither merited by the recipient, nor necessary for an adequate start in life, nor compatible with any conceivable coherent account of equal life chances, it's being bequeathed substantial amounts of wealth by one's parents. Historically, as Danny Dorling notes, 'most people have inherited very little because their parents had very little to leave. To see inheritance as normal we have to have the mindset and beliefs about other people that only the aristocracy once had' – the mindset that says that it's so imperative to avoid living like ordinary people if you possibly can, that it's fair to leave money to one's children to spare them that fate (Dorling, 2015, p 31). But because the belief that one has the right to bequeath to one's children whatever one has left remains so strong (it's 'the most natural thing in the world', for David Cameron), it is worth reframing the policy. Dead people don't benefit from bequeathing wealth. Neither do they hurt when they are taxed on what they bequeath. But their children do benefit from receiving it. So tax all inheritance not as if it were in any way a tax on dying, but as if it were any other kind of *income*, means-tested according to the circumstances of the receiver. If the receiver is below the income tax threshold, don't tax their inheritance unless it is such to take them above that threshold. If they are already wealthy, tax them heavily. Redistribute the revenue raised from this to pay for the following.

2. Investing more in pre-school support for families on low incomes

New Labour's Sure Start initiative, begun in 1998 – the provision of centres (with slight variations in the four UK countries) offering a range of services to families with young children in areas of deprivation – is certainly open to critique (Lister, 2006). It can seem crassly instrumental, if viewed as a scheme to co-opt parents into the creation of a better-skilled workforce. But even if that is part of the motivation, that should not define the very idea. Initiatives like these use economic resources to invest in cultural capital – so combining redistribution with elements of recognition. They can be a way of acknowledging the weight of the 'bedtime stories' factor, facilitating parents in helping prime their kids for school learning: holding longer conversations, reading to them, encouraging them to raise their own questions and exercise their curiosity. But, two things: these programmes need to be bigger. And they should treat the beneficiaries not as future capable, healthy contributors to the economy or compliant citizens (Featherstone, 2014, p 317), but as individuals with an independent interest in their own current and future flourishing. All such schemes should engage with parents not as feckless, precarious victims to be spoon fed expert wisdom, but as individuals skilled with their own expert insights into the interests of their own children.

3. Redistributing childcare

Childcare can be seen as a relationship good, and also as what some call a 'distribuendum' (Brighouse and Swift, 2014; Gheaus, 2016). That is, it is something we might include in the goods to be distributed according to our understanding of social justice. This has various advantages, all of which echo points made in Chapter Two. It identifies potential value in caring relationships in themselves; it combines insights from either side of the care versus justice relationship; it firmly situates the quality of domestic relations within the purview of social justice; and it recognises the central place of childcare in any nation's economy. It might seem odd to think that childcare, as a relationship, can be redistributed. This might make it sound like money, or corn. But there are different kinds of distribuenda, as the contrast between economic, social and cultural capital makes clear. Not all things unevenly distributed in society, or distributable along fairer lines, are material goods. Redistributing childcare would be as crucial a step as any in ensuring greater equivalence between family circumstances, and thus in children's life chances. It does this in two ways: by enabling parents to work, and by providing access to early-years resources of education and care that disadvantaged families might otherwise go without. There are various ways in which it might be done. One obvious contender is the provision of universal childcare for all up to a certain age (Roberts, 2014) – a policy usually promoted on the basis of its economic benefits (see, for example, Ben-Galim, 2011), but which can equally be couched in terms of a step towards more equal life chances.

These are just piecemeal, localised suggestions; that's partly their point. Of course there are other possibilities, ranging from the closely specific – the targeting of funds to help those from less well-off backgrounds overcome the often prohibitive costs of qualifying to work in some higher-status professions, such as the law and journalism; the elimination of nepotism in the allocation of internships – to the more ambitious, like the introduction of a universal citizen's income. Each will carry a baggage of debate as to its efficacy and fairness. Each, though, would need to be accompanied by an overall change in the pitch and presumptions of public discourse on what we mean by giving every child a fair start in life – and what exclusive privileges many will need to loosen their grip on, in order to make that aspiration even something like a reality.

SIX

Seven conclusions

This book has looked at how inequality runs in families, and at ways in which that can be seen as unfair. We defined 'family' in a deflationary way, in Chapter Two: as (following Archard) 'a multigenerational group, normally stably co-habiting, whose adults take primary custodial responsibility for the dependent children'. One reason for doing so was to avoid some of the heftier ideological debates that set in as soon as the family is brought up. I have not tried to 'sell' the family – this kind of multigenerational group –as a general force for either good or bad, but rather to look at some of the implications it has for wider questions of fairness. In concluding, it seems worth restating seven key claims that have been made in the chapters in between. Here, they will come across like slogans. But there is a story behind each, in the previous chapters. So while each is contentious, and contested, there are good grounds for defending them.

1. **What happens within and between families is, without question, a matter of social justice.**

2. **Issues of social justice and issues of care should be addressed together, rather than on an either/or basis.**

3. **Equality of opportunity cannot be genuinely realised without being addressed in conjunction with equality of condition (or outcome).**

4. **More equal societies (in terms of equality of condition) have better rates of social mobility.**

5. **Although lack of social mobility is a symptom of class fate, promoting social mobility is not the solution to the problems and injustices with which class fate is associated.**

6. **Social mobility should be seen as an upshot of social justice – of a society where everyone is treated fairly – rather than a route to it.**

7. **To tackle how inequality runs in families requires both tackling inequality and challenging common-sense assumptions about the extent of parents' rights to advantage their children over others.**

Concerns about social mobility – raised loud and often in the work of the Social Mobility Commission – are vital to hear. They have shed strong, searching light on the drastically unequal contours of societies like the UK in the 21st century. What we should not do is assume that social mobility itself is the answer to those concerns, or that it will, by itself, stop inequality running in families.

References

Ainley, P. (2016) *Betraying a generation: how education is failing young people*. Bristol: Policy Press.

Almond, B. (2006) *The fragmenting family*. Oxford: Clarendon Press.

Archard, D. (2003) *Children, family and the state*. Aldershot and Burlington: Ashgate.

Archard, D. (2010) *The family: a liberal defence*. Basingstoke: Palgrave Macmillan.

Baier, A. (1987) 'The need for more than justice', *Canadian Journal of Philosophy*, supplementary vol 13: 14-56.

Baker, J. (1987) *Arguing for equality*. London and New York, NY: Verso.

Barry, B. (2005) *Why social justice matters*. Cambridge: Polity Press.

Ben-Galim, D. (2011) *Making the case for universal childcare*. London: Institute for Public Policy Research.

Benn, M. and Downs, J. (2016) *The truth about our schools: exposing the myths, exploring the evidence*. London: Routledge.

Bennett, A. (2014) 'Fair play', *London Review of Books*, 19 June. Available at www.lrb.co.uk/v36/n12/alan-bennett/fair-play (accessed 22 July 2014).

Bloodworth, J. (2016) *The myth of meritocracy: why working-class kids get working-class jobs*. London: Biteback.

Boliver, V. and Byrne, D. (2013) 'Social mobility: the politics, the reality, the alternative', *Soundings*. 55: 50-9.

Bourdieu, P. (1997; orig. 1983) 'The forms of capital', trans. R. Nice, in A. H. Halsey, H. Lauder, P. Brown and A. Stuart Wells (eds) *Education: Culture, Economy, Society*. Oxford: Oxford University Press.

Breen, R. (2010) 'Social mobility and equality of opportunity: Geary Lecture Spring 2010', *The Economic and Social Review*, 41(4): 423-8.

Brighouse, H. (2002) *Egalitarian liberalism and justice in education*. London: Institute of Education.

Brighouse, H. and Robeyns, I. (eds) (2010) *Measuring justice: primary goods and capabilities.* Cambridge: Cambridge University Press.

Brighouse, H. and Swift, A. (2009) 'Legitimate parental partiality', *Philosophy & Public Affairs*, 37(1): 43–80.

Brighouse, H. and Swift, A. (2014) *Family values: the ethics of parent-child relationships.* Princeton, NJ: Princeton University Press.

Brown, G. (2010) 'We can break the glass ceiling', *The Guardian*, 15 January. Available at www.theguardian.com/commentisfree/2010/jan/15/aspiration-mobility-middle-class-labour (accessed 12 December 2015).

Butler, I. and Drakeford, M. (2013) 'Children's rights as a policy framework in Wales', in J. Williams (ed) *The United Nations Convention on the Rights of the Child in Wales*, Cardiff: University of Wales Press.

Calder, G. (2007) *Rorty's politics of redescription.* Cardiff: University of Wales Press.

Calder, G. (2015) 'Brighouse and Swift on the family, ethics and social justice', *European Journal of Political Theory*, DOI:10.1177/1474885115587119.

Calder, G. (2016) 'Family autonomy and class fate', *Symposion: Theoretical and Applied Inquiries in Philosophy and Social Sciences* 3(2): 131–49.

Cameron, D. (2015) 'Tories pledge to take family homes out of inheritance tax', 11 April. Available at http://www.theguardian.com/politics/2015/apr/11/tories-pledge-to-take-family-homes-out-of-inheritance-tax (accessed 12 April 2015).

Carers UK (2015) 'Valuing carers 2015'. Available at www.carersuk.org/news-and-campaigns/campaigns/we-care-don-t-you/value-my-care/valuing-carers-2015 (accessed 5 December 2015).

Carey, T. (2014) *Taming the tiger parent.* London: Robinson.

Cass, B. (2007) 'Exploring social care: applying a new construct to young carers and grandparent carers', *Australian Journal of Social Issues*, 42(2): 241–54.

Chambers, D. (2001) *Representing the family.* London: Sage.

Chambers, D. (2012) *A sociology of family life.* Cambridge: Polity Press.

Channel 4 News (2012) 'Osborne unveils £10bn benefits cuts package', 8 October. Available at www.channel4.com/news/osborne-unveils-10bn-benefits-cut-package (accessed 3 February 2016).

Chowdry, H. Greaves, E. and Vignoles, A. (2010) *The pupil premium: assessing the options*. London: Institute for Fiscal Studies.

Clark, L. (2007) 'Thousands of young carers being robbed of childhood', *Daily Mail*, 10 May. Available at www.dailymail.co.uk/news/article-453794/Thousands-young-carers-robbed-childhood.html (accessed 6 December 2015).

Clark, T. (2014) *Hard times: the divisive toll of the economic slump*. New Haven, CT: Yale University Press.

Clarke, H. and O'Dell, L. (2014) 'Disabled parents and normative family life: the obscuring of the lived experiences of parents and children within policy and research accounts', in J. Ribbens-McCarthy, C. Hooper and V. Gillies (eds) *Family troubles: exploring changes and challenges in the family lives of children and young people*. Bristol: Policy Press.

Clegg, N. (2010) 'Inequality becomes injustice when it is passed on, generation to generation', *The Guardian*, 23 November. Available at www.theguardian.com/commentisfree/2010/nov/22/inequality-injustice-nick-clegg (accessed 20 December 2015).

Clegg, N. (2011) 'Foreword by the Deputy Prime Minister', in HM Government, *Opening doors, breaking barriers – a strategy for social mobility*. London: Cabinet Office.

Cooper, K. and Stewart, K. (2013) *Does money affect children's outcomes? Summary*. York: Joseph Rowntree Foundation.

Corak, M. (2012) 'How to slide down the Great Gatsby Curve: inequality, life chances, and public policy in the United States', 5 December. Available at http://milescorak.com/2012/12/05/how-to-slide-down-the-great-gatsby-curve-inequality-life-chances-and-public-policy-in-the-united-states (accessed 5 July 2014).

Corak, M. (2013) 'Income inequality, equality of opportunity and intergenerational mobility', *Journal of Economic Perspectives*, 27(3): 79-102.

Crawford, C., Johnson, P., Machin, S. and Vignoles, A. (2011) *Social mobility: a literature review*. London: Department for Business, Innovation and Skills.

Crawford, C., Macmillan, L. and Vignoles, A. (2014) *Progress made by high-attaining children from disadvantaged backgrounds*. London: Social Mobility and Child Poverty Commission.

Davies, J., Berger, B. and Carlson, A. (1993) *The family: is it just another lifestyle choice?* London: Institute for Economic Affairs.

Donnelly, L. (2008) 'Dame Carol Black on sick-note Britain', *Sunday Telegraph*, 9 March. Available at www.telegraph.co.uk/news/uknews/1581193/Dame-Carol-Black-on-sick-note-Britain.html (accessed 3 February 2016).

Dorling, D. (2014) *Inequality and the 1%*. London and New York, NY: Verso.

Dorling, D. (2015) *Injustice: why social inequality still persists*. Bristol: Policy Press.

Eno, B. (2016) 'This much I know', *Observer* magazine, 27 March. Available at www.theguardian.com/lifeandstyle/2016/mar/26/brian-eno-i-dont-get-much-of-a-thrill-out-of-spending-money (accessed 27 March 2016).

Equality and Human Rights Commission (2015) *Is Wales fairer? The state of equality and human rights in 2015*. Cardiff: Equality and Human Rights Commission.

Erickson, M. (2015) *Class war: the privatization of childhood*. London and New York, NY: Verso.

Exley, S. (2016) 'Education and learning', in H. Dean and L. Platt (eds) *Social advantage and disadvantage*. Oxford: Oxford University Press.

Featherstone, B. (2014) 'Working with fathers: risk or resource?', in J. Ribbens-McCarthy, C.-A. Hooper and V. Gillies (eds) *Family troubles? Exploring changes and challenges in the family lives of children and young people*. Bristol: Policy Press.

Feinstein, L. (2003) 'Inequality in the early cognitive development of British children in the 1970 cohort', *Economica*, 70: 73-97.

Fischer, T. (2007) 'Parental divorce and children's socio-economic success', *Sociology*, 41(3): 475-95.

Fishkin, J. L. (1983) *Justice, equal opportunity and the family*. New Haven, CT and London: Yale University Press.

Fraser, N. (1997) 'From redistribution to recognition? Dilemmas of justice in a "postsocialist" age', in N. Fraser, *Justice interruptus: critical reflections on the 'postsocialist' condition*. New York, NY and London: Routledge.

Fraser, N. (2013) 'Struggle over needs: outline of a socialist-feminist critical theory of late-capitalist political culture', in N. Fraser, *Fortunes of feminism*. London and New York, NY: Verso.

Fry, R. (2016) 'For first time in modern era, living with parents edges out other living arrangements for 18-34-year-olds', Pew Research Center, 24 May. Available at www.pewsocialtrends. org/2016/05/24/for-first-time-in-modern-era-living-with-parents-edges-out-other-living-arrangements-for-18-to-34-year-olds (accessed 24 May 2016).

Full Fact (2012) 'Freedom of information shows no evidence for thousands of "never worked" families'. Available at https:// fullfact.org/economy/freedom-information-shows-no-evidence-thousands-never-worked-families (accessed 3 February 2016).

Gheaus, A. (2009) 'How much of what matters can we redistribute? Love, justice, and luck', *Hypatia*, 24(4): 63-83.

Gheaus, A. (2014) 'What is the value of (even fair) equality of opportunity in an unjust society?', 19 March. Available at http:// justice-everywhere.org/old-blog/what-is-the-value-of-even-fair-equality-of-opportunity-in-an-unjust-society (accessed 15 January 2016).

Gheaus. A. (2016) 'Hikers in flip-flops: luck egalitarianism, democratic equality and the distribuenda of justice', *Journal of Applied Philosophy*, DOI: 10.1111/japp.12198

Gill, N. (2016) 'Why UKIP would bring back grammar schools', *ClickonWales*, 2 May. Available at www.clickonwales.org/2016/05/ why-ukip-would-bring-back-grammar-schools (accessed 3 May 2016).

Gilligan, C. (1982) *In a different voice: psychological theory and women's development*. Cambridge, MA: Harvard University Press.

Gilligan, C. (1986) 'Remapping the moral domain', in T. Heller, M. Sosna and D. Wellbury (eds) *Reconstructing individualism: autonomy, individuality, and the self in western thought*. Stanford, CA: Stanford University Press.

Glass, D. (1953) 'Introduction', in D. Glass (ed) *Social mobility in Britain*. London: Routledge and Kegan Paul.

Goldthorpe, J., with Llewellyn, C. Payne, C. (1987) *Social mobility and class structure in modern Britain*, 2nd edn. Oxford: Clarendon Press.

Goldthorpe, J. (2012) 'Understanding – and misunderstanding – social mobility in Britain: the entry of the economists, the confusion of politicians and the limits of educational policy'. Available at www.spi.ox.ac.uk/fileadmin/documents/PDF/Goldthorpe_Social_Mob_paper_01.pdf (accessed 15 December 2015).

Goldthorpe, J. (2016) 'Decades of investment in education have not improved social mobility', *The Observer*, 13 March. Available at www.theguardian.com/commentisfree/2016/mar/13/decades-of-educational-reform-no-social-mobility (accessed 13 March 2016).

Graham, G. (2014) 'Working class children must learn to be middle class to get on in life, government advisor says', *Daily Telegraph*, 3 March. Available at www.telegraph.co.uk/education/10671048/Working-class-children-must-learn-to-be-middle-class-to-get-on-in-life-government-advisor-says.html (accessed 13 December 2015).

Hall, S. and O'Shea, A. (2015) 'Common-sense neoliberalism', in S. Hall, D. Massey and M. Rustin (eds) *After neoliberalism? The Kilburn manifesto*. London: Lawrence & Wishart.

Hanley, L. (2016) *Respectable: the experience of class*. London: Allen Lane.

Harle, E. (2013) 'The new prince and his 2000 birthday buddies', Left Foot Forward, 23 July. Available at http://leftfootforward.org/2013/07/the-new-prince-and-his-2000-birthday-buddies (accessed 5 March 2016).

Hart, B. and Risley, T. R. (1995) *Meaningful differences in the everyday experiences of young American children*. Baltimore, MD: Brookes Publishing.

Hellen, N. (2015) 'Dim Tims hoard the best jobs', *The Sunday Times*, 26 July, p 5.

Hennessy, P. (2013) 'Confidence in British monarchy at all-time high, poll shows', *Daily Telegraph*, 27 July. Available at www.telegraph. co.uk/news/uknews/theroyalfamily/10206708/Confidence-in-British-monarchy-at-all-time-high-poll-shows.html (accessed 5 March 2016).

Hern, A. (2012) '"Four generations of families where no-one has ever had a job"? Probably not, Mr Grayling', *New Statesman*, 13 December. Available at www.newstatesman.com/economics-blog/2012/12/four-generations-families-where-no-one-has-ever-had-job-probably-not-mr-grayl (accessed 3 February 2016).

Hills, J. (2015) *Good times, bad times: the welfare myth of them and us.* Bristol: Policy Press.

HM Government (2011) *Opening doors, breaking barriers – a strategy for social mobility*. London: Cabinet Office.

Hochschild, A. (2012; orig. 1989) *The second shift: working families and the revolution at home*. New York, NY: Penguin.

Honneth, A. (1992) 'Integrity and disrespect: principles of a conception of morality based on the theory of recognition', *Political Theory*, 20(2): 187-201.

Hope, C. (2010) 'Middle classes told to stop using Sure Start', *Daily Telegraph*, 11 August. Available at www.telegraph.co.uk/news/politics/david-cameron/7937248/Middle-classes-told-to-stop-using-Sure-Start.html (accessed 13 December 2013).

Hoskins, K. and Barker, B. (2014) *Education and social mobility: dreams of success*. London: Trentham Books.

Jones, O. (2013) Interview on Start the Week, BBC Radio 4, 6 June. Available at www.bbc.co.uk/programmes/b02yjf15 (accessed 3 March 2016).

Jones, O. (2011) *Chavs: the demonization of the working class*. London and New York, NY: Verso.

Kittay, E. F. (1999) *Love's labor: essays on women, equality and dependency*. New York, NY and London: Routledge.

Koster, O. (2008) 'The "terrible legacy" of the children growing up in families who haven't worked for generations', *Daily Mail*, 10 March. Available at www.dailymail.co.uk/news/article-528877/The-terrible-legacy-children-growing-families-havent-worked-generations.html (accessed 3 February 2016).

Kynaston, D. (2015) *Modernity Britain 1957-62.* London: Bloomsbury.

Lanning, T., Bradley, L., Darlington, R. and Gottfried, G. (2013) *Great expectations: exploring the promises of gender equality.* London: Institute for Public Policy Research.

Lareau, A. (2011) *Unequal childhoods: class, race and family life*, 2nd edn. Berkeley: University of California Press,

Lipsey, D. (2015) 'The meritocracy myth – and what ever happened to the old dream of a classless society?', *New Statesman*, 27 February–5 March: 23.

Lister, R. (2006) 'Children (but not women) first: New Labour, child welfare and gender', *Critical Social Policy*, 26(2): 315-36.

Littler, J. (2013) 'Meritocracy as plutocracy', *New Formations*, 80-81: 52-72.

McCann, J. (2016), '12 year old Amy Barbour on being a young carer: I don't want people to pity me', *Daily Express*, 24 January. Available at www.express.co.uk/life-style/life/636159/Young-Carers-Awareness-Day-January-2016 (accessed 25 January 2016).

MacDonald, R. (2015) 'The power of stupid ideas: "three generations that have never worked"'. Available at https://workingclassstudies.wordpress.com/2015/05/11/the-power-of-stupid-ideas-three-generations-that-have-never-worked (accessed 3 February 2016).

MacDonald, R. and Shildrick, T. (2012) 'Exposed: the myth of a culture of worklessness', *The Guardian,* 14 December. Available at www.theguardian.com/commentisfree/2012/dec/14/worklessness-culture-myth-exposed (accessed 3 February 2016).

MacIntyre, A. (1999) *Dependent rational animals: why human beings need the virtues.* Chicago and La Salle, IL: Open Court.

Machin, S., Gregg, P. and Blanden, J. (2005) *Intergenerational mobility in Europe and North America.* London: Sutton Trust.

Macmillian, L. (2011) *Measuring the intergenerational correlation of worklessness*. Bristol: Centre for Market and Public Organisation. Available at www.bristol.ac.uk/media-library/sites/cmpo/migrated/documents/wp278.pdf (accessed 3 February 2016).

Mandler, P. (2016) 'Educating the Nation: III. Social Mobility', *Transactions of the Royal Historical Society*, 6th series, 26-forthcoming.

Marquand, D. (2013) *Mammon's kingdom: an essay on Britain, now*. London: Allen Lane.

Marshall, G., Swift, A. and Roberts, S. (1999) *Against the odds? Social class and social injustice in industrial societies*. Oxford: Oxford University Press.

Milburn, A. (2015), 'Social mobility – the key to a fairer Scotland'. Speech at David Hume Institute, 2 November. Available at www.davidhumeinstitute.com/next-seminar-21-october-2015-internationalising-scottish-business (accessed 20 February 2016).

Moore, S. (2016) 'Never mind a level playing-field – private schools bawl when anyone ventures near the electric fence'. *The Guardian G2*, 2 June, p 5. Available at www.theguardian.com/commentisfree/2016/jun/01/suzanne-moore-private-education-level-playing-field-electric-fence (accessed 2 June 2016).

Moullin, S. (2015) 'The demography of predistribution: families, economic inequalities and social policies', in C. Chwalisz and P. Diamond (eds) *The predistribution agenda: tackling inequality and supporting sustainable growth*. London and New York, NY: I. B. Tauris.

Neil, A. (2011) 'Does a narrow social elite run the country?', *BBC Magazine*. Available at www.bbc.co.uk/news/magazine-12282505 (accessed 23 December 2015).

Noggle, R. (forthcoming) 'Children's rights', in G. Calder, J. De Wispelaere and A. Gheaus (eds) *The Routledge Handbook of Childhood and Children*, London and New York, NY: Routledge.

Nussbaum, M. C. (2000) *Sex and social justice*. Oxford: Oxford University Press.

Nussbaum, M. C. (2001) *Women and human development*. Cambridge: Cambridge University Press.

O'Dell, L., Crafter, S., Abreu, G. and Cline, T. (2010) 'Constructing "normal childhoods": young people talk about young carers', *Disability & Society* 25(6): 643-55.

OECD (Organisation for Economic Co-operation and Development) (2010) 'A family affair: intergenerational social mobility across OECD countries'. Available at www.oecd.org/tax/public-finance/chapter%205%20gfg%202010.pdf (accessed 11 December 2015).

Okin, S. M. (1989) *Justice, gender and the family*. New York, NY: Basic Books.

Olsaretti, S. (2013) 'Children as public goods?', *Philosophy and Public Affairs* 41(3): 226-58.

O'Neill, M. (2016) 'Creating a more equal future', in A. Harrop and E. Wallis (eds) *Future left: can the left respond to a changing society?* London: Fabian Society.

ONS (Office for National Statistics) (2010) *Social trends* 40. Available at http://webarchive.nationalarchives.gov.uk/20160105160709/http://ons.gov.uk/ons/rel/social-trends-rd/social-trends/social-trends-40/index.html (accessed 10 April 2016)

ONS (Office for National Statistics) (2011a) '2011 census'. Available at www.ons.gov.uk/census/2011census (accessed 16 September 2015).

ONS (2011b) 'General lifestyle survey: 2011'. Available at www.ons.gov.uk/peoplepopulationandcommunity/personalandhouseholdfinances/incomeandwealth/compendium/generallifestylesurvey/2013-03-07 (accessed 10 April 2016).

ONS (2015) 'Families and households: 2015 (statistical bulletin)'. Available at www.ons.gov.uk/peoplepopulationandcommunity/birthsdeathsandmarriages/families/bulletins/familiesandhouseholds/2015-11-05 (accessed 21 January 2016).

Osborne, G. (2013) Interview, The Andrew Marr Show, BBC1. Available at www.youtube.com/watch?v=YObFTW8pH_E (accessed 12 January 2014).

Parsons, T. (1956) 'The American family: its relations to personality and to the social structure', in T. Parsons and R. F. Bales, *Family socialisation and interaction process*. London: Routledge and Kegan Paul.

Plato (1993; orig. c. 370 BC) *Republic*, trans. Robin Waterfield. Oxford: Oxford University Press.

Putnam, R. D. (2015) *Our kids: the American dream in crisis*. New York, NY: Simon & Schuster.

Raftery, A. E. and Hout, M. (1993) 'Maximally maintained inequality: expansion, reform, and opportunity in Irish education, 1921-75', *Sociology of Education* 66(1): 41-62.

Rawls, J. (1999) *A theory of justice*, revised edn. Cambridge, MA: Harvard University Press.

Reay, D. (2016) 'Social mobility, a panacea for austere times: tales of emperors, frogs, and tadpoles', in P. Brown, D. Reay and C. Vincent (eds) *Education and social mobility*. London and New York, NY: Routledge.

Roberts, Y. (2014) 'Three words could end confusion and financial distress for parents: free universal childcare', *The Guardian*, 31 March. Available a: www.theguardian.com/money/she-said/2014/mar/31/three-small-words-could-end-financial-distress-and-confusion-for-parents-free-universal-childcare (accessed 1 April 2014).

Robinson, N. (2013) 'All infants in England to get free school lunches', BBC News, 17 September. Available at: http://www.bbc.co.uk/news/uk-politics-24132416 (accessed 3 February 2016).

Rogers, A. and Clements, B. (1985) *The moral basis of freedom*. Exeter: Victoria Books.

Rutter, J. and Stocker, K. (2014) *Childcare costs survey 2014*. London: Family and Childcare Trust.

Sacks, J. (2016) 'The good society is one where we all have the chance to flourish', Thought for the Day, BBC Radio 4, 19 February. Text available at www.rabbisacks.org/the-good-society-is-one-where-we-all-have-the-chance-to-flourish-thought-for-the-day (accessed 10 May 2016).

Saunders, P. (1996) *Unequal but fair? A study of class barriers in Britain*. London: Institute of Economic Affairs.

Saunders, P. (2010) *Social mobility myths*. London: Civitas.

Savage, M., Cunningham, N., Devine, F., Friedman, S., Laurison, D., McKenzie, L., Miles, A., Snee, H. and Wakeling, P. (2015) *Social class in the 21st century*. London: Pelican.

Sayer, A. (2005) *The moral significance of class*. Cambridge: Cambridge University Press.

Sayer, A. (2009) 'Contributive justice and meaningful work', *Res Publica*, 15(1): 1-16.

Sayer, A. (2016) 'Review essay: what is the question?', *Soundings*, 62: 167-75.

Sen, A. (1995) *Inequality reexamined*. Oxford: Oxford University Press.

Sen, A. (2009) *The idea of justice*. London: Allen Lane.

Shaddock, L. (2016) 'It's time to rein in executive pay', Equality Trust website, 5 January. Available at www.equalitytrust.org.uk/its-time-rein-executive-pay (accessed 6 January 2016).

Shildrick, T. (2012) 'Are "cultures of worklessness" passed down through the generations?', Joseph Rowntree Foundation, 13 December. Available at www.jrf.org.uk/report/are-cultures-worklessness-passed-down-generations (accessed 3 February 2016).

Social Mobility and Child Poverty Commission (2015a) *Elitist Britain?*. London: Social Mobility and Child Poverty Commission.

Social Mobility and Child Poverty Commission (2015b) *State of the nation 2015: social mobility and child poverty in Great Britain*. London: Social Mobility and Child Poverty Commission.

Stewart, K. (2016) 'The family and disadvantage', in H. Dean and L. Platt (eds) *Social advantage and disadvantage*. Oxford: Oxford University Press.

Stratton, A. (2011) 'David Cameron: broken society is top of my political agenda', *The Guardian*, 15 August. Available at www.theguardian.com/uk/2011/aug/15/david-cameron-riots-broken-society (accessed 10 April 2016).

Swift, A. (2003) *How not to be a hypocrite: school choice for the morally perplexed parent*. London and New York, NY: Routledge.

Tawney, R. H. (1920) *The acquisitive society*. New York, NY: Harcourt and Brace.

Tawney, R. H. (1964) *Equality*, 4th edn. London: George Allen & Unwin.

Thatcher, M. (1987) Interview, *Woman's Own*, 23 September. Available at www.margaretthatcher.org/document/106689 (accessed 21 January 2016).

Tilly, C. (1998) *Durable inequality*. Berkeley, CA: University of California Press.

Tinsley, M. (2014) *Parenting alone: work and welfare in single parent households*. London: Policy Exchange.

Tomlin, P. (2016) 'Saplings and caterpillars: trying to understand children's well-being', *Journal of applied philosophy*, DOI: 10.1111/japp.12204.

Tronto, J. (1994) *Moral boundaries: a political argument for an ethic of care*. New York, NY and London: Routledge.

Tronto, J. (2010) 'Creating caring institutions: politics, plurality, and purpose', *Ethics & Social Welfare* 4(2): 158-71.

United Nations (1948) 'Declaration of human rights'. Available at www.un.org/en/universal-declaration-human-rights/index.html (accessed 16 January 2016).

United Nations (1989) 'The convention on the rights of the child'. Available at www.unicef.org/crc (accessed 16 January 2016).

Vallentyne, P. and Lipson, M. (1989) 'Equal opportunity and the family', *Public Affairs Quarterly*, 3(4): 29-47.

White, S. (2007) *Equality*. Cambridge: Polity Press.

Wilkinson, R. and Pickett, K. (2010) *The spirit level: why equality is better for everyone*, rev. edn, London: Penguin.

Willetts, D. (2011) *The pinch: how the baby boomers took their children's future – and why they should give it back*. London: Atlantic Books.

Willis, P. (1993; orig. 1978) *Learning to labour: how working class kids get working class jobs*. Farnham and Burlington, VT: Ashgate.

Wright, E. O. (2015) *Understanding class*. London and New York, NY: Verso.

Young, I. M. (2011; orig. 1990) *Justice and the politics of difference*. Princeton, CT: Princeton University Press.

Young, M. (1958) *The rise of the meritocracy*. London: Thames and Hudson.

Young, M. (2001) 'Down with meritocracy', *The Guardian*, 29 June. Available at www.theguardian.com/politics/2001/jun/29/comment (accessed 3 March 2016).

Index